T0373819

Official Cambridge Exam Preparation

PREPARE

WORKBOOK WITH DIGITAL PACK

C1 LEVEL 8

Greg Archer | Second Edition

Cambridge University Press
www.cambridge.org/elt

Cambridge Assessment English
www.cambridgeenglish.org

Information on this title: www.cambridge.org/9781108913348

© Cambridge University Press and Cambridge Assessment 2022

First published 2022

20 19 18 17 16 15 14 13 12 11 10 9 8 7

Printed in Poland by Opolgraf

A catalogue record for this publication is available from the British Library

ISBN   978-1-108-91334-8   Workbook with Digital Pack
ISBN   978-1-108-91333-1   Student's Book with eBook
ISBN   978-1-108-91335-5   Teacher's Book with Digital Pack

CONTENTS

1 WHAT ARE YOU LIKE?

VOCABULARY AND READING
PERSONALITY

1 Match the adjectives in the box to the definitions. There are two definitions that you do not need to use.

> conscientious   introverted
> self-conscious   trustworthy

1 someone who's focused, follows the rules and takes a lot of care over their studies or work ....
2 someone who often feels nervous or uncomfortable about themselves ....
3 someone who's keen to be with other people and is socially confident ....
4 someone who's willing to consider other ideas that are different to their own ....
5 someone who's shy and prefers to spend time alone ....
6 someone who can be relied on and will always keep a secret ....

2 Which adjectives do the two remaining definitions from Exercise 1 describe?

e .... v ....
o .... – m .... d ....

3 Correct the mistakes in the phrasal verbs in bold.

For most teenagers, it sometimes feels impossible not to [1] **clash to** your parents. The generation gap is strikingly clear at this point in life, and it becomes more difficult for parents and children to [2] **relate for** each other. For you, perhaps the way in which they talk to you often [3] **comes away** as negative, as if they are trying to control aspects of your life that you want to keep private. Your parents, on the other hand, find themselves in a position where their child now prioritises relationships with their friends, rather than with immediate family and so they naturally [4] **feel left off**. Their child no longer [5] **relies to** them for guidance and companionship, and this can be difficult to take.

1 ....
2 ....
3 ....
4 ....
5 ....

4 What does it take to become somebody's close friend? Make a list of the important factors, then read the article on the opposite page quickly to compare your ideas.

....
....
....
....

5 What is the best heading for each paragraph?

A Grading friendships ....
B Investigating shared thought processes ....
C Moving from theory to reality ....
D Setting the minimum requirements ....
E Researching an abstract concept ....

6 Read the sentences. Write A if the information is correct, B if it is incorrect or C if the information isn't given.

1 Researchers have devised an absolute method for measuring friendship. ....
2 All of the surveys that were initially sent contained identical questions. ....
3 It is extremely common to become close to people who do the same job as you. ....
4 The University of California study asked participants to describe videos to their friends. ....
5 Close friends can lose touch despite having spent lots of time together. ....
6 Most people meet their best friends at school or at work. ....

7 Match the highlighted words and phrases in the article to the meanings.

1 choose from a group for special focus ....
2 causes something to be examined further ....
3 clear and certain ....
4 people who are the same age or have the same social position or the same abilities as other people in a group ....
5 not willing or slow to do something ....

TIME FOR **MAKING FRIENDS**

1 Would you say it is easy to distinguish between a friend and a close friend? Being able to categorise *closeness* in any concrete way not only seems unnecessary, but also problematic. Where would you even start? Recent studies from the University of Kansas suggest that it might be possible to objectively state the points at which people move up the friendship scale. They have investigated how long it initially takes to be simply called a friend and how long it then takes to become a close friend.

2 First of all, the researchers sent an online survey to 355 adults who had recently moved into a new town or city, asking them to picture someone they had met since they had arrived there and how their friendship had developed. The participants were then asked to quantify how many hours they had spent with that friend and to grade the level of friendship: acquaintance, casual friend, friend, or close friend. At the same time, 112 University of Kansas students completed the same survey about two people they had encountered since starting college a few weeks previously. The researchers followed up after four and seven weeks to see how the friendships had evolved.

3 Their results suggest that it takes around 40 to 60 hours of time spent in each other's company to form a casual friendship and 80 to 100 hours to move into the friend category. However, if you have recently met someone with whom you would like to become a close friend, be prepared to work for it, as you will need a minimum of 200 hours in their company. The research also showed that, when people move between friendship stages, they'll double or triple the amount of time they spend with someone within the space of a month. Given that previous research elsewhere has found that a person's brain is capable of handling about 150 friendships at once, it begs the question: do people actually do anything in life apart from starting, developing and maintaining friendships?

4 And to what extent do friends think in similar ways? It may seem obvious that this is the case, and many people would feel reluctant to qualify or quantify how it happens, but another group of researchers has shown that science will often have the answer. In a recent study, a group of cognitive scientists at the University of California put to one side obvious, traditional ideas of friendship and looked into the role that neurology plays. They asked 279 students to complete an online survey which asked them to single out individual peers who they would classify as friends. Then, while the participants were watching a series of video clips of, for example, an astronaut's view of Earth, the researchers scanned their brains to find out whether they shared similar brain patterns to those of their friends. The results suggest that friends share similarities in how they process and notice the world around them, and this seems to play a part in achieving the shared social interaction that can make or break a friendship. If you don't think alike, the chances of a friendship developing are fewer.

5 Perhaps this explains why, for everyone, there are people who we thought were close friends, but one day we realise they have slipped out of our lives. Perhaps we just haven't put the hours in. Perhaps it's a combination of the two. It's hard to be certain, as each friendship is unique and impossible to manufacture. I personally would argue that if you do want to be someone's best friend, you need to spend time with them, and lots of it. And if you spot that someone has friendship potential, be proactive. If you are in the same school, suggest some time doing homework together or playing sports after class. If you work together, suggest sharing a lunch break. Making the first move is a clear signal to people that you are interested in becoming their friend and provides you with that valuable time to see if you think in similar ways. Neurologically speaking, of course.

GRAMMAR
PAST TENSE REVIEW

1 Choose the correct options.

1 Philip *has gone / had gone* to the shops, but he'll be back later.

2 I *dropped / have dropped* my ticket while I *boarded / was boarding* the train yesterday.

3 My dad *met / had met* his best friend at school, nearly forty years ago.

4 Millie's so forgetful – she *has asked / had asked* me six or seven times if I'm going to her party.

5 The exam wasn't easy, but I *had prepared / prepared* really well, so I'm hopeful of a good grade.

6 When he *went / was going* to his previous school, he *would often walk / was often walking* home on his own.

2 Complete the sentences with the verbs in brackets in the correct form.

1 Your mother _____ (work) really hard lately – it's no surprise she's tired.

2 Since I left college, I _____ (find) it difficult to stay in touch with my old classmates.

3 I saw Simon earlier today, when he _____ (run) in the park.

4 Most people found the exam awful, but I _____ (not think) it was too difficult.

5 By the time I left primary school, I _____ (change) my best friend at least ten times.

6 Whenever Marco saw Luis, he _____ (tease) him about the time he fell asleep in class.

3 Read the first part of the story and correct the mistakes in bold with the correct form of the verbs.

From the first time I [0] **had seen** him, I knew that Spencer and I were going to be friends. We bumped into each other as he [1] **walked** into school for his first day, and I decided to say 'hi'. I [2] **studied** there for my whole life up to that point and had no worries or fears about going in, so perhaps it just [3] **was seeming** to him like I was incredibly confident. When I looked at him, he turned away almost immediately. It was pretty clear that Spencer was feeling a little bit nervous about being the new guy.

'Hi,' I said, 'I'm Katya.'

'Hello,' he said, 'I'm Spencer. I'm new here.'

I laughed and explained that I [4] **would realise** the moment I saw him that it was his first day and promised to help him to get to know the place. It was certainly a good time to join the school; recently, the principal [5] **invested** a lot of money in the buildings, which was a huge improvement on the way it [6] **was used to being**. Pretty much every day, the students [7] **have complained** about the old furniture, the lack of technology and so on. So, they finally did something about it. After I told Spencer all this, he laughed and said that his old school [8] **hadn't even been having** enough chairs for the students to sit on in some classrooms.

0	*saw*	5	
1		6	
2		7	
3		8	
4			

4 Complete the second part of the story with the verbs in the box in the correct form.

> appear   believe   fix   gain   happen   hope
> move   walk   wonder   ~~work~~

'Was it really that bad?' I asked. Apparently so. The technology in most classrooms [0] *hadn't been working* for years. There was a huge hole in the roof of the gym, which no one [1] _____ . The students generally [2] _____ that a high percentage of the teachers [3] _____ any sort of qualification as lessons were slow and pointless. Understandably then, before Spencer [4] _____ to this area, he [5] _____ to change schools for ages. 'I can't believe that it [6] _____ , finally,' he said. Things [7] _____ to be looking up for Spencer.

At this point, I noticed that my best friend Cassie [8] _____ towards us. Spencer went white.

'Hello, Lisa,' he said, nervously.

'Hello, Spencer', she replied, coldly.

I wondered to myself … why did he call her Lisa? And why didn't she correct him?

5 Which of the following sentences are incorrect? Why?

1 My best friend used to live in Madeira when she was really young.

2 My best friend would live in Madeira when she was really young.

3 Every summer, we used to go on family holidays to Madeira.

4 Every summer, we would go on family holidays to Madeira.

⊙ 6 Correct the mistakes in the sentences or put a tick by any you think are correct.

1 I have made so many new friends when I went to university last year. _____

2 There was a huge park near our house where I use to go with my parents. _____

3 Until I became more confident, I would often get too nervous to speak to new people. _____

4 I haven't seen Maria for ages – it's like she is just disappeared! _____

5 It had been such an interesting day until Adam turned up. _____

6 In the nineteenth century, people had often lived with their grandparents. _____

7 When my parents got married, they had been together for less than three months. _____

8 During his childhood, Peter usually would visit his cousins once a week. _____

VOCABULARY
ADJECTIVE AND ADVERB SUFFIXES

1 Choose the correct options.

1 Mira is incredibly *sensible / sensitive*, so make sure you don't say anything to upset her.

2 I can't stand *selfish / narrow-minded* people who can't accept others for who they are.

3 When people are older, they are generally more *respectful / responsible* with money.

4 David is completely *fearless / bossy* – he'd already done a bungee jump by the time he was fourteen!

5 You're so *chatty / childish* with everyone – you'd make a great interviewer on TV.

6 With all this bad news around us, it's sometimes difficult to be *optimistic / realistic* about the future.

2 Change these nouns into adjectives and add them to the correct columns in the table.

care	child	clumsiness	competition	disappointment	energy	enthusiasm	fascination	fuss
hope	horror	knowledge	liberty	misery	origin	reliability	responsibility	style	support

-able	-al	-ed	-ible	-ic	-ish	-ive	-less/-ful	-y

3 Complete the sentences with the adjectives from Exercise 2.

1 I studied a lot, so I'm _____ of a good grade.

2 It's really difficult to have a relaxing game of tennis with my sister because she's so _____ .

3 My kids are amazing, but they're so _____ . I always end the day completely worn out.

4 My brother has always been _____ by the possibility of travelling the world on his own.

5 Alessandro's very _____ , so I can guarantee he will be there on time.

6 You're so _____ – that's the third time you've knocked over a glass today!

7 I get on better with people who have _____ points of view. I hate it when people discriminate against others.

8 Daniil is amazingly _____ – he designs and makes all his own clothes.

4 Complete the sentences with the words in brackets in adjective form.

0 You'll end up losing friends if you keep acting so *bad-temperedly* (bad temper) when you're tired.

1 My grandmother can talk _____ (knowledge) about so many different subjects – she's really intelligent.

2 I would _____ (happiness) do anything for my best friend.

3 I'd love to move out of my family home and live by myself. _____ (reality), though, it's not going to happen until I'm a lot older.

4 Annette is going to be famous one day – she can sing so _____ (beauty).

5 Paolo's brother was _____ (falseness) accused of stealing stationery from the office.

6 After his latest dating disaster, Ben asked himself _____ (misery), 'Why does this always happen to me?'

5 For questions 1–8, read the article below. Use the word given in capitals at the end of some of the lines to form a word that fits in the gap in the same line. The first word is given as an example.

THE SECRET TO A LONG, HAPPY FRIENDSHIP

The most important factor in a friendship is having **(0)** *reasonable* expectations of each other. Respect for personal space and boundaries is vital. As long as you understand that your friend is your friend – and not your pet – you should, for the most part, get on **(1)** _____ well. So many people fall out with good friends after a **(2)** _____ argument in which one person feels let down, or someone hasn't shown **(3)** _____ , and suddenly that bond between two people is broken. Always ask yourself: is it worth losing a good friend because of a **(4)** _____ argument?

If you value your friendships, you need to be **(5)** _____ and admit you will not always see eye to eye. You are, after all, two different people, and there is no point in adopting a **(6)** _____ attitude. Being a good friend is about being **(7)** _____ and showing that you will always be there for them, even if you don't **(8)** _____ agree with their views or actions. Remember, treating friends honestly is essential if you want to remain close for a long time.

REASON

FANTASTIC

CHILD

KIND

POINT

REAL

JUDGEMENT
SUPPORT

NECESSARY

LISTENING

1 You will hear two friends discussing a film about a friendship. Which films have you seen that deal with friends or friendship? What made the films enjoyable/disappointing?

....

....

....

....

2 Look at question 1 in Exercise 4 and underline the key words.

3 In which of the following conversations do the speakers show agreement with each other?

1 A: I really enjoyed that. Did you?
  B: Yeah, what a great way to spend a Saturday evening.

2 A: It's really easy to lose yourself in a film like that, particularly one that's so full of colour, and vivid.
  B: Mmm, it was a real pleasure for the eyes.

3 A: … you just know that what you're watching on screen is exactly what's happening to millions of people all over the world, every day.
  B: Did you find that?

4 A: … there were probably too many lucky coincidences in the storyline for me.
  B: I'd probably give you that.

🔊 **4** Listen to the first part of the conversation and answer the question below.
01

Extract 1
You hear two friends discussing a film about friendship.

1 Which aspect of the film do the friends disagree about?
  A The film was realistic and mirrored real life.
  B The plot had several problematic aspects.
  C The setting was visually attractive.

🔊 **5** Listen to the first part of the conversation again and answer the question below.
01

2 Which aspect of the film did the girl particularly enjoy?
  A It addressed its subject matter in an intelligent way.
  B It encouraged the audience to forget about outside issues.
  C It lasted for the optimum length of time.

6 Read the extract below and underline the sections that show why the incorrect options in Exercise 5 are wrong.

I'd probably give you that. But no movie is perfect, and if the aim of this film was simply to provide some welcome distraction for the viewers, I'd say the director certainly achieved that. Sometimes, you want to watch a movie that makes you think, and at other times you really just need something else. I can't believe we were in the cinema for well over two hours, but you know you've enjoyed yourself if it feels like far less.

 7 You will hear two more extracts. For questions 3–6, choose the answer (A, B or C) which fits best according to what you hear. There are two questions for each extract.
🔊 02

Extract 2
You hear two friends discussing university accommodation.

3 What is the boy's concern about living with friends?
  A It would distract him too much from his studies.
  B It would make him feel excessively homesick.
  C It would be more expensive than living on campus.

4 Why does the girl give the example of her sister?
  A to convince the boy to move in with his friends
  B to express sympathy with the boy's difficult decision
  C to encourage the boy to focus on his studies

Extract 3
You overhear a girl showing her friend a photo of her family.

5 What does the girl most appreciate about the photo?
  A It perfectly captures her grandmother's personality.
  B It inspires her to see her family more often.
  C It displays her family in a moment of contentment.

6 When the boy talks about photography, he is suggesting that people
  A should try to limit the number of pictures they take.
  B are able to find a connection between humour and memory.
  C can use photos to build personal connections with others.

READING AND USE OF ENGLISH

1 Read the article in Exercise 5 quickly. What advice would you give the writer?

....

....

2 Underline the four words that are most similar to each other in meaning.

> beginning   creation   development   growth   mode
> production   style   type   variety   world

3 Which of the answers from Exercise 2 best complete the sentences?

1 My preferred .... of transport is the train.
2 He's got a really interesting .... of teaching.
3 He has a .... of smart clothes to wear to work.
4 I'm not the .... of student who always completes homework on time.

4 Read the first sentence of the article in Exercise 5 again. Why is C the correct option?

....

....

5 Read the article and decide which answer (A, B, C or D) best fits each gap.

What can I do to stop
being so shy?

I have always been an introverted **(0)** _type_ of person. I never feel confident when I meet new people. I also tend to ask silly questions and act in a **(1)** .... way, but only because I don't want to show that I **(2)** .... so nervous. It sometimes means that I'll come **(3)** .... as arrogant, but actually quite the opposite is true. I remember at one party, I was so focused on being friendly that I walked **(4)** .... into a door frame and almost knocked myself out.

But I'm not as bad as I was. When I was little, I **(5)** .... hide behind my parents' legs, even if a family member I knew **(6)** .... well came to visit, and sometimes **(7)** .... into tears if they tried to talk to me. It still **(8)** .... me down from time to time, especially when I meet someone new who I want to become friends with.

0 A style	**B** variety	**C** type	**D** mode
1 A conscientious	**B** self-conscious	**C** convincing	**D** trustworthy
2 A 've felt	**B** 've been feeling	**C** would feel	**D** 'd felt
3 A across	**B** about	**C** away	**D** by
4 A clumsy	**B** clumsiness	**C** clumsily	**D** clumsier
5 A would	**B** used	**C** did	**D** could
6 A particularly	**B** specially	**C** mainly	**D** specifically
7 A surge	**B** rush	**C** open	**D** burst
8 A gets	**B** has	**C** pushes	**D** hits

6 Look at the title of the article in Exercise 10. What do you think the article is about?

....

....

7 Read the article in Exercise 10 quickly and compare its ideas with your predictions.

8 Look at question (0) in Exercise 10. Which of the options is correct? Why?

A that   **B** because   **C** how   **D** so

9 Look at question (1). Which of the options is correct? Why?

A now   **B** then   **C** when   **D** here

....

....

10 For questions 1–8, read the text below and think of a word that best fits each gap. Use only one word in each gap.

CAN'T TALK – I'M ON THE STAIRS!

It seems strange to think, if you consider **(0)** .... easily and immediately we can chat with friends and family these days, that communication has not always been this accessible.

Until mobiles came along, people were generally content with their landline telephones. Back **(1)** ...., if someone wanted to phone a friend, it meant returning to the same spot in their house each time and holding a heavy plastic handset to their ear, **(2)** .... was never particularly comfortable for anyone. People today frequently walk long distances while on a call, but they certainly didn't use **(3)** .... Not when their phone was plugged **(4)** .... the wall, anyway …

This could lead to difficulties **(5)** .... twentieth-century teenagers, as they often found **(6)** .... impossible to have private conversations. If they weren't lucky enough to have a phone in their own rooms, teenagers **(7)** .... have to speak to their friends in the hallway, the living room or the kitchen – and clashing **(8)** .... their parents was often the result.

2 THE BIGGER THE BETTER?

VOCABULARY AND READING
CITIES

1 Put the letters in the correct order to make words related to cities.

1 PRATRONTS SLINK _____
2 HHIG-SIRE _____
3 ENERG CAPESS _____
4 BRUSUBS _____
5 LENSYED APEDPLUTO _____
6 LETRICED _____
7 GRIN DOAR _____
8 ASPIREDESTINED _____
9 BRAUN PRAWLS _____
10 USSML _____

2 Match the definitions to the words from Exercise 1.

1 natural environments within a city, e.g. parks _____
2 a tall, modern building with many floors _____
3 a building or place that is in bad condition and not cared for _____
4 an area that has been adapted so that traffic is not allowed to pass through it _____
5 an area on the edge of a large town or city where people who work in the town or city often live _____
6 a very poor and crowded area of a city _____
7 a main road that goes around a town or city, allowing traffic to avoid the busy centre _____
8 describes an area where a large number of people live closely together _____
9 connections that provide road or rail access between different places _____
10 the spread of a city into the area around it, often without planning permission _____

3 Complete the sentences with the words from Exercise 1.

1 Many investors have become very rich by buying _____ buildings and transforming them into high-quality studio apartments.
2 It takes ages to get to my cousin's house because of the limited _____ where she lives.
3 Young people are generally attracted to life in the _____ city centre, where they have plenty of opportunities to meet new people.
4 It's no wonder the _____ in Mexico City extends so far in every direction – more than 20 million people live there.
5 In the 21st century, it is vital for governments to work together to ensure that poor people no longer live in _____, anywhere in the world.
6 I'm so grateful for the _____. If it wasn't there, traffic in the city centre would be even worse than it is now.
7 When I was growing up, we didn't have a great deal of space in the _____ building where my family lived, but we certainly had some amazing views.
8 The council are currently considering whether the streets around my area should be _____ to make it safer for children to walk to school.

4 Look at the photo on the opposite page. What do you think the people might be doing?

5 Read the article on the opposite page quickly. What is unusual about the role the young people play?

6 Read the article again. For questions 1–6, choose the answer (A, B , C or D) which you think fits best according to the text.

1 What does 'this' in line 9 refer to?
   A how citizens' needs are assessed
   B what largely drives urban development
   C what many find appealing about city life
   D how people perceive change in their surroundings

2 How did Jette feel on returning to cities where he had once lived?
   A dissatisfied with how their growth excluded certain groups
   B disappointed in how much bigger they had grown
   C confused about the popularity of car-free zones
   D concerned about how similar to each other they were becoming

3 In the third paragraph, what is Jette's main observation about young people, according to the writer?
   A how familiar they are with their neighbourhoods
   B how stimulated they are by playing online computer games
   C how willing they are to adapt to regulations
   D how free they are in their approach to problem-solving

4 In the fourth paragraph, the writer expresses how Jette
   A thought city planners often waste huge sums of money.
   B thought young residents' suggestions are not given enough credit.
   C tends not to consider his subject in enough depth.
   D thought different age groups tend to have conflicting preferences.

5 In the fifth paragraph, the writer shows how Jette felt
   A grateful to the teachers of the young people he talked to.
   B in agreement with the young people's philosophy.
   C shocked at how little he knew in comparison to the interviewees.
   D amused by the young people's descriptions of what they had imagined.

6 The writer makes the point that urban planning should
   A focus on the knowledge and experience of local authorities.
   B consider the psychological aspects of new developments.
   C encourage co-operation from international governments.
   D invite contributions from people with different strengths.

BRINGING IN THE NEW BLOOD

Journalist Michael Taylor meets Nicolas Jette, architect of a modern approach to urban planning and design.

Cities around the world are often said to develop naturally and organically, adapting themselves to the constantly changing wishes of the people who live there. Or so the theory goes. While this romantic idea may have been true many centuries ago, many cities today have grown according to strict calculations and criteria. The requirements of their residents still feature on any list of planning specifications, but they are primarily redesigned and built with a singular aim in mind – profit. The result of this is that the main voices in the design process are always those of adults, for whom the city functions according to patterns of work and money-generating social interaction. Young people, however, are often left out of the planning process.

Urban design agency Shape Shifter is aiming to change this. Its CEO, Nicolas Jette, believes that modern cities must evolve with a more inclusive sense of social responsibility in mind. 'My parents travelled internationally a lot when I was growing up, so I spent my adolescence continually moving between many different cities around the world,' he remembers. Frequently, if he went back to a city years after leaving it, he was frustrated at how any expansion failed to show concern for its younger residents. For example, there were often an increased number of pedestrianised areas, but who are these really for? Generally, they exist in areas where people go to work or to spend money, neither of which feature heavily in teenagers' lives.

Jette was determined to bring young people into the urban development process. Initially, he found inspiration in Blockbuilders, a not-for-profit organisation based in the UK that allows younger teenagers to engage with real-world city design through the online game *Minecraft*. He noticed the way in which children as young as eleven were able to analyse, re-imagine and transform the layout of their own local areas, and could visualise their ideal result without being too concerned about how difficult it might prove to be in real life. This is in clear contrast to the way in which adults who design cities do so with a sense of caution – restricted by rules, budgets and anticipated objections.

Once Jette began interviewing teenagers of all ages, he realised how valuable their ideas could be – if anyone would listen. He asked them what issues there were in their cities and what changes they would like to see. Of course, there were some inevitable suggestions, such as increasing the number of skate parks available. But they also raised some valuable points that even he hadn't previously considered. For example, many cities have spent millions on establishing modern public transport links, but the aim is often to encourage people out of their cars and onto trams, trains and buses – and here lies the problem. As his interviewees explained, this often discourages city-dwellers from cycling, which, in their opinion, should actually be the main alternative to private car travel.

Jette also noted that the young people he spoke to all made it a priority to have greater access to green spaces wherever possible, providing him with numerous welcome suggestions about how he could create such facilities for them in densely populated cities. Sometimes, they might produce detailed descriptions of outdoor recreation zones in which to enjoy the natural environment. At other times, their innovative proposals would be based on project work done at school or college. They introduced him, for example, to Vincent Callebaut, the Belgian architect and designer of futuristic eco-districts, whose work many of the interviewees had researched or studied. After Jette went away to carry out his own research into the work of Callebaut, he found that this was all he needed to be convinced of the worth of his interviewees' ideas.

The *top-down* approach to urban planning is when political decision-makers take charge, whereas *bottom-up* requires the involvement of residents on street level. There is certainly a powerful argument that, as Jette puts it, 'you have to go and knock on doors, find the information you need, and convince the people at the top to make those changes.' While I feel it would be ill-advised to dismiss the expertise available in local and national governments, this type of enthusiasm and sense of purpose is an equally valuable resource.' He is planning to take his research to the relevant authorities around the world, hoping to persuade them that his recommendations are the most important factor in the future mental health of the residents of any city.

7 Underline the parts of the text which tell you the answers to Exercise 6.

8 Match the highlighted words in the text to the definitions.

1 a way of enjoying yourself when you are not studying or working
2 plans of how much money will be earned and spent
3 not wise and likely to cause problems
4 include someone or something as an important part
5 the people who live in a city

GRAMMAR
COMPARATIVES AND SUPERLATIVES

1 Tick the correct sentence in each pair.

1 A Most people agree that it's much harder to learn how to drive in a city than in the countryside.
B Most people agree that it's much hardlier to learn how to drive in a city than in the countryside.

2 A Paris is easily the most beautiful city I've ever visited.
B Paris is easy the most beautiful city I've ever visited.

3 A The journey from London to Manchester is far more quicker by train than by coach.
B The journey from London to Manchester is far quicker by train than by coach.

4 A I've had the worst time trying to find a new flat – I haven't liked any that I've seen so far.
B I've had the worse time trying to find a new flat – I haven't liked any that I've seen so far.

5 A Tobias lives in the most unusually decorated apartment you'll ever see.
B Tobias lives in the most unusual decorated apartment you'll ever see.

6 A We really should visit other cities in this country frequentlier.
B We really should visit other cities in this country more frequently.

7 A He's more patient than he used to be.
B He's more patienter than he used to be.

8 A I wouldn't stay there; it's by far the least interesting part of the city.
B I wouldn't stay there; it's far the least interesting part of the city.

9 A Now that it runs on time, I'm more slightly enthusiastic about taking the metro to work.
B Now that it runs on time, I'm slightly more enthusiastic about taking the metro to work.

10 A Sara is more and more and confident each time I see her.
B Sara is more and more confident each time I see her.

2 Correct the mistakes in the sentences.

1 The river boat is by far best way to see some of the city's architecture.

2 I thought getting into town by car was bad, but it is even worst on the bus.

3 The staircase design is one of the elements more interesting in my house.

4 Most of the people in my family can cook more successful than me.

5 My new bed is far too comfortable than the one I used to have.

6 Sorry I'm late – your new apartment is farer away than I had expected.

3 Complete the sentences with a double comparative phrase, using the word in brackets.

0 Ben has been acting *less and less strangely* (strange) since he started seeing his old friends again – thank goodness!

1 When an area of a city becomes more popular, it also becomes _____ (affordable) for young people.

2 I'm getting _____ (concerned) that they're going to build yet another high-rise office block close to our road.

3 The delays in completing the roadworks on the ring road are becoming _____, (frequent) so hopefully it'll be finished soon.

4 When they suddenly realised they shared a passion for interior design, Andrea and Paula started discussing the idea of sharing a flat _____ (enthusiastic).

4 Rewrite the sentences using the *the ... the ...* structure.

0 When the roads become icy, driving is more difficult.
The icier the roads become, the more difficult driving is.

1 If you try harder, you'll be more successful.

2 When the weather is good, the city looks less unattractive.

3 You'll be able to afford a nicer flat by saving more money.

4 As he gets older, he becomes less kind.

5 Choose the correct options.

1 The government has decided to make all public transport free for *elder / older* people.

2 Moving into a flat-share with my brother was one of the *better / best* ideas I have ever had.

3 Roni would happily go into the city centre if there were *less / fewer* people out shopping.

4 According to the *last / latest* statistics, over 80% of people in Spain now live in cities.

5 Increased investment in fibre-optic cables has made it *more easy / easier* for people in remote areas to access superfast broadband.

6 Architects often forget the golden rule in creating functional buildings: the *simpler / simplier*, the better.

7 It's *less comfortable / less convenient* to get to work from my new apartment – I now have to take three buses.

8 *The most / Most* students prefer watching a movie at home than at the cinema.

VOCABULARY

BUILDINGS AND PLACES: IDIOMS

1 Choose the correct options.

1 I think I've *broken / found* the glass ceiling at work – I've finally been promoted.

2 I know you're angry, but be careful not to *burn / build* your bridges when you speak to her.

3 David always goes *to / into* town when he has a party – they're so much fun.

4 The architect's plans aren't set in *concrete / stone*, so feel free to make any additional suggestions.

5 My sister hit the *roof / ceiling* when she saw that the dog had been digging in her garden.

6 The best thing about visiting my grandmother is the way she always makes us feel *at / like* home.

7 Sylvie has thrown out the expensive new wardrobe we bought for her. Our money went *down / to* the drain.

8 Michael and Thomas got on like a *house / home* on fire when they first met, and they do everything together now.

9 When I leave home, all I want is to *have / keep* a roof over my head, and then I'll be happy.

10 Even the best musicians hit a *stone / brick* wall sometimes and can't make a song work.

2 Match the definitions to the idioms from Exercise 1.

1 like each other very much and become friends very quickly ....

2 be completely wasted ....

3 have somewhere to live ....

4 be very difficult/impossible to change ....

5 reach a point where it becomes difficult to continue ....

6 do something very enthusiastically, often spending a lot of money ....

7 get extremely angry ....

8 get to a more important position at work despite unofficial and unfair restrictions ....

9 be comfortable/relaxed ....

10 destroy all possible ways of going back to a previous situation ....

3 Rearrange the words in bold to form an idiom. There is one extra word you do not need to use.

0 Tessa is refusing to speak to Jo any more. She says that Jo **burnt has her down bridges** after their last big argument. *has burnt her bridges*

1 They spent all that money on trying to develop the city centre, but most of it has **the gone drain broken down**. I certainly can't see any improvements.
....

2 When we were trying to sell our house, my parents really **town the went to**. They bought flowers for every room and hired a professional cleaning company.
....

3 People who rent apartments are often charged a deposit before moving in, but there's nothing **in set up stone** regarding how much that should be.
....

4 After making a good start to negotiations, it seems the council and the residents have **wall a hit the brick** over plans to build a new park in the city.
....

4 Complete the second sentence so that it means the same as the first sentence, using the word given. Use between three and six words, including the word given.

1 When Antonio flooded the bathroom by accident, his mum got so angry. **HIT**
Antonio's mum ....
after he flooded the bathroom by accident.

2 I'm usually confident and comfortable when I'm walking around a big city. **AT**
Usually, I .... when I'm
walking around a big city.

3 My classmates and I really enjoy each other's company, which helps when we work on a project together. **ON**
My classmates and I get
........................., which helps when
we work on a project together.

4 Many people find it impossible to get the work promotion they believe they deserve. **BREAK**
Many people find it impossible to
.... at work.

5 As long as I have somewhere to live, I don't care whether I'm in the city or the countryside. **OVER**
As long as I have ....,
I don't care whether I'm in the city or the countryside.

6 The council spent a huge amount of money on that Bank Holiday parade. **TO**
The council really ....
on that Bank Holiday parade.

7 Our plans might change in the future, but we're happy here for now. **SET**
Our plans ...., but
we're happy here for now.

8 After that argument with her boss, I think he is unlikely to trust her again. **BRIDGES**
I think she .... with
her boss after that argument.

9 We wasted all our savings when we bought that useless car. **DOWN**
All our savings ....
when we bought that useless car.

10 It seemed like my career stopped progressing after I went part-time. **HIT**
My career seemed ....
after I went part-time.

THE BIGGER THE BETTER?   13

WRITING
INFORMAL EMAILS OF ADVICE

» SEE *PREPARE TO WRITE* BOX, STUDENT'S BOOK PAGE 18

1 **Which of the following sentences would not be acceptable in an informal email? How could the more formal ones be improved?**

   1 Fantastic news that you're going to be studying architecture at university!
   2 Not sure if I've told you, but I'm planning to do exactly the same thing next year.
   3 Anyway, speak soon.
   4 Who knows when we might meet again?
   5 Many thanks for your email; I hope to answer your enquiries below.
   6 Looking forward to seeing you soon.
   7 I was thinking about you just last week!
   8 Once again, I greatly appreciate your interest in my opinion.
   9 It's wonderful that you've got in touch after so long.
   10 Why not have a think and let me know next week?

2 **Are the acceptable answers in Exercise 1 more likely to appear at the beginning or the end of the email? Write *B* (beginning) or *E* (end).**

   1 .... 3 .... 6 .... 9 ....
   2 .... 4 .... 7 .... 10 ....

3 **Complete the email with the phrases in the box.**

> How's it going?   in the next day or two
> Looking forward to   Never mind
> only lives down the road   No idea why, though
> No wonder really,   presumably
> Shame you couldn't

Hi Paco,

¹ _____ Good to hear that you're coming to stay with your aunt in Cambridge next month. She ² _____ from me, so you can come round to mine really easily. It'll be amazing! I'll have a think about where we should go ³ _____ – I'm studying so hard at the moment, I've got tons of revision to do. ⁴ _____ come in a few weeks' time, when my exams will be over.

⁵ _____ meeting up with you in a few days.

Speak soon,

Dani

4 **Complete this email with the remaining four phrases from the box in Exercise 3.**

Hey Alice,

Lovely to hear from you, and glad you've got that great new job. ¹ _____, you were always the clever one at school. So, if the offices are in Seville, you'll be looking for a new place to live soon, ² _____? It's such a great place – I've always thought about living there, but it never really happened. ³ _____, but you can't always have everything you want in life, can you? ⁴ _____, I'm sure I'll get to visit you loads, anyway.

Congratulations,

Sara

5 **Which of the phrases from the box in Exercise 3 have a similar meaning to the phrases 1–8?**

   0 Can't wait to hang out with   *Looking forward to seeing*
   1 I'm not a bit surprised.   ....
   2 How are things?   ....
   3 Pity there's no way you could   ....
   4 Not to worry   ....
   5 is only around the corner   ....
   6 I imagine   ....
   7 Can't think why, though   ....
   8 over the next couple of days   ....

6 **Find examples of the following strategies used in Dani's and Sara's emails.**

   1 paying a compliment ....
   2 exaggeration ....
   3 using exclamation marks ....
   4 asking questions / checking details ....

7 Match the sentence halves. Then underline the structures used to give advice.

1 If I were you, I'd avoid,
2 I tend to have dinner quite late, so you might want to
3 If you give me some ideas about what you'd like to do,
4 The hotels are quite expensive here, so you could consider
5 My parents really liked you when they met you, so how about
6 Do make sure that you
7 The weather is going to be great next week, so why not
8 Don't worry too much if

a I'll come up with a few suggestions for you.
b getting here in the morning, as I'll probably be out.
c leave enough time to get from one flight to another at the airport.
d you decide not to come in the end – I know how busy you are.
e think about coming then, instead?
f get a snack or something on your way here.
g finding a decent youth hostel instead.
h staying with us while you're here?

1	3	5	7
2	4	6	8

8 Make notes to answer the following questions.

1 Why do people decide to redecorate their bedrooms by themselves?

2 What do you think are the advantages/disadvantages of doing so?

3 Why would somebody's parents not want them to redecorate?

4 What advice would you give someone who is trying to persuade their parents to allow them to redecorate their bedroom?

9 Read the following task and add any other ideas to your notes in Exercise 8.

> This is part of an email you received from your friend Dominique.
>
> > … I'm thinking of redecorating my bedroom as it has looked the same for eight years now, but I'm not sure my parents will let me. Do you think it would be a good idea for me to redecorate? How should I convince my parents to allow me to do it?

10 Complete the first part of the email with four appropriate phrases from this unit.

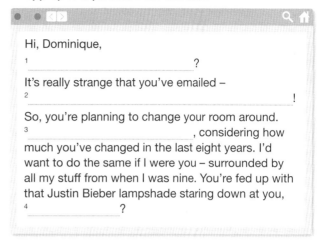

Hi, Dominique,

1 _____ ?

It's really strange that you've emailed –
2 _____ !

So, you're planning to change your room around.
3 _____, considering how much you've changed in the last eight years. I'd want to do the same if I were you – surrounded by all my stuff from when I was nine. You're fed up with that Justin Bieber lampshade staring down at you,
4 _____ ?

11 Write the rest of the email, using structures to give advice from Exercise 7.

3 ALL IN ONE PIECE

VOCABULARY AND READING

THE HUMAN BODY

1 Answer the questions.

What is

1 the medical term for *breathing out*? ....

2 a word that describes an absence of feeling in a body part? ....

3 the collective noun for arms and legs? ....

4 an informal word for bacteria and viruses? ....

5 a place in your body where two bones are connected? ....

6 an action that might prevent you from breathing? ....

2 Choose the correct options.

1 I'm feeling a bit *poorly / poor*, but I don't think I need to see a doctor.

2 My grandmother's always in pain. Some days, she can't even bend her *joints / nerves*.

3 Milla started to panic when she saw her little boy *inhaling / choking* on his dinner.

4 Upper back pain may be caused by problems with your *germs / spine*.

5 It's really painful to look down – I must have a trapped *nerve / numb* in my neck.

6 *Left-hand / Left-handed* people find it uncomfortable using most scissors.

7 Cover your face when you sneeze, otherwise you'll spread your *germs / lungs* everywhere.

8 Billy came back from his run covered in *sweat / nerves*.

3 Complete the sentences with one word.

1 Passive smoking is when non-smokers .... the fumes of someone else's cigarette.

2 I can't feel my right arm – it's completely .... I must have slept on it last night.

3 Apart from a limited number of fish and snails, mammals are the only living things which have ....

4 When someone loses an arm or a leg, they can be replaced with an artificial ....

5 Although I'm .... , I play tennis with my left.

6 That sauna was ridiculous – I didn't stop .... from the moment I got in.

7 When the weather is cold, my grandfather gets terrible pains in his .... He can hardly bend his elbows or knees.

8 Your brain sends signals through a system of .... to other parts of the body.

4 Write three pieces of advice about exercise for people in their late teens. Then read the article on the opposite page and see if any of your points are included.

....
....
....

5 Read the article again and answer the questions with *M* (Maria), *R* (Remi), *A* (Adam) or *S* (Suki).

1 Who suggests writing down a timetable of physical activity? ....

2 Who suggests a quick, reduced workout can maintain fitness levels if there is a lack of time available? ....

3 Who says that they are taking steps to control the ageing process? ....

4 Who recommends avoiding exercise at times of restricted physical health? ....

5 Who encourages a particular group of people to react positively to changes to a schedule? ....

6 Who mentions using a reward as the basis for motivation? ....

7 Who advises against putting pressure on yourself to take pleasure in exercise? ....

8 Who mentions the value of correct preparation for an exercise session? ....

6 Choose the answer (A, B or C) which you think fits best according to the text.

1 What does Maria mean by 'qualities' in line 18?
   A personal characteristics unrelated to study
   B techniques for improving mental health
   C additional study time outside of the classroom

2 What point does Remi emphasise?
   A that people can easily lose interest due to poor exercise technique
   B that people rarely have enough time to exercise
   C that people are often too impatient to see their fitness levels improve

3 How does Adam characterise his feelings about exercise?
   A He regrets how physically uncomfortable it is.
   B He sees how it can provoke a negative response.
   C He feels sorry for anyone who suffers an injury.

4 Why does Suki mention her younger self?
   A to show how successful she has always been
   B to illustrate how easily she used to find winning races
   C to establish a contrast with her current approach

7 Match the highlighted words and phrases in the article to the meanings.

1 start or develop as the result of something ....

2 a great variety; a wide range ....

3 a system or ordered way of doing things ....

4 be the first person to do something that solves a problem or improves a situation ....

5 when something happens completely unexpectedly ....

KEEPING FIT AND LOVING IT

Four people share their ideas about the ways in which teenagers can most benefit from exercise.

MARIA, DOCTOR

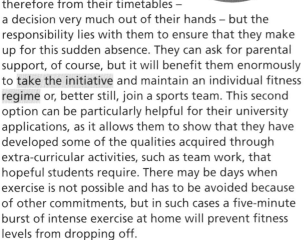

Older teenagers often find that they have reached a point in life where they have to choose between exercise and socialising or studying. This results partly from the disappearance of sport from the curriculum and therefore from their timetables – a decision very much out of their hands – but the responsibility lies with them to ensure that they make up for this sudden absence. They can ask for parental support, of course, but it will benefit them enormously to take the initiative and maintain an individual fitness regime or, better still, join a sports team. This second option can be particularly helpful for their university applications, as it allows them to show that they have developed some of the qualities acquired through extra-curricular activities, such as team work, that hopeful students require. There may be days when exercise is not possible and has to be avoided because of other commitments, but in such cases a five-minute burst of intense exercise at home will prevent fitness levels from dropping off.

ADAM, WELLNESS CONSULTANT

We live in a world where there is so much pressure on us to look and feel as great as possible. It's easy to feel disappointed if your exercise regime isn't doing what you had hoped it would – like all that effort has been for nothing. Give yourself a break. People in their late teens have all manner of pressures related to time and study that they haven't experienced before, so this is a good moment in life to develop time management skills. Make sure you come up with a plan, of course, which maps out your fitness schedule alongside your studies, whether on paper or digitally. But the key is to move away from this whenever you need to. Believe me, I have every sympathy for anyone who finds doing exercise a real pain – I am no different. After all, an intense workout doesn't necessarily equal fun and enjoyment, so give yourself some flexibility in how much you can achieve.

REMI, PERSONAL TRAINER

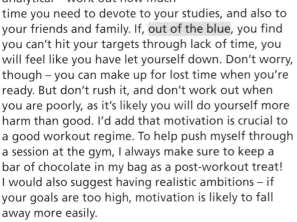

Most of what you can achieve in terms of physical fitness actually stems from where you are mentally. A vital aspect of success is making sure you take control of your life. Be completely analytical – work out how much time you need to devote to your studies, and also to your friends and family. If, out of the blue, you find you can't hit your targets through lack of time, you will feel like you have let yourself down. Don't worry, though – you can make up for lost time when you're ready. But don't rush it, and don't work out when you are poorly, as it's likely you will do yourself more harm than good. I'd add that motivation is crucial to a good workout regime. To help push myself through a session at the gym, I always make sure to keep a bar of chocolate in my bag as a post-workout treat! I would also suggest having realistic ambitions – if your goals are too high, motivation is likely to fall away more easily.

SUKI, ATHLETE

When I was younger, I could just walk onto the athletics track and – bang! – launch myself into a competitive race there and then, often winning. But doing that now would be extremely foolish (even though I'm still not exactly old). I've become increasingly aware of how vital it is to warm up first, to get the blood pumping and provide my muscles with more oxygen. In one sense, it's purely so I can give myself every opportunity to win that race – and it's certainly helped me to do that. But it's also about the fact that building good habits is fundamental to staying in peak condition. As you get older, your body starts responding less well to immediate bursts of activity, so I'm trying to get ahead of that now. If I'm being completely honest, I don't think I'll ever get used to the early starts on training days, though I have found a useful life hack to tackle that. If I put my phone in my kit bag on the other side of the bedroom, I have no choice but to drag myself out of bed to turn the alarm off, and seeing my running kit immediately puts me in the mood for some intense exercise.

GRAMMAR
MODALS

1 Read the sentences and choose the correct function of the modal verb.

1 You've just finished a 10 km run? Wow, you must be exhausted!
  A permission **B** advice **C** obligation **D** speculation/deduction

2 You must make sure that you hand in your registration card on time.
  A permission **B** advice **C** obligation **D** speculation/deduction

3 You don't need to worry about coming home early – it's a beautiful evening.
  A permission **B** advice **C** lack of obligation **D** speculation/deduction

4 You can ask me anything you want at our appointment tomorrow.
  A permission **B** advice **C** obligation **D** speculation/deduction

5 You should make more of an effort to cut down on red meat.
  A permission **B** advice **C** obligation **D** speculation/deduction

6 You can't be hungry! We only had dinner half an hour ago.
  A permission **B** advice **C** lack of obligation **D** speculation/deduction

7 You can't invite more than ten people to your party, I'm afraid.
  A permission **B** advice **C** obligation **D** speculation/deduction

8 You ought to leave your bike somewhere else – this is a common place for thieves.
  A permission **B** advice **C** obligation **D** speculation/deduction

2 Choose the correct options. Sometimes both are correct.

1 You *mustn't / don't have to* take this medication unless your doctor has prescribed it to you.

2 I *need to / must* remember to call the surgery and get my blood test results.

3 Peter just told me that he *has to / can* go into hospital for an operation on his knee.

4 If you don't finish your science homework this evening, you *will have to / must* come back to it tomorrow.

5 These pills are a little difficult to swallow, but thankfully you *don't have to / don't need to* take them for more than a fortnight.

6 If you're not feeling well, you *may / can* go to the nurse's office.

3 Complete the sentences with the words *should, ought, can* or *could* in the correct form.

1 They .... become members of that gym as they're under eighteen.

2 I'm not sure if I .... reply to this email. What would you do?

3 .... I ask you for a little help, if it's not too much trouble?

4 We .... to hurry up, or else we're going to miss the start of class.

5 Chrissie thinks she's going to get an offer from Harvard, but I don't think she .... get too excited about it.

6 You .... tell other people about my news if you want. I don't mind who knows about it.

4 Complete the sentences with three words in each gap.

0 It's not possible that this is the right way to the gym.
  This ...*can't be the*... right way to the gym.

1 It's extremely important that I remember to call my grandmother today.
  I .... call my grandmother today.

2 I have no doubt that my dad knows that he's being really unfair.
  My dad .... unfair he's being.

3 If you tidy your room before you leave, I'll let you stay out after 10.
  You .... after 10 this evening if you tidy your room first.

4 Peter is new to the job – it's our responsibility to help him out.
  Peter is new to the job – we .... sure we help him out.

5 If the traffic is okay, there's a chance we'll be home before midnight.
  If the traffic is okay, we .... before midnight.

6 Maybe John doesn't know who to ask.
  John .... who to ask.

7 You're not allowed to enter – it's a restricted area.
  That is a restricted area and ....

8 I don't think it's a very good idea to use that brand of shampoo to wash your hair.
  You really .... else to wash your hair with.

5 Correct the mistakes in the sentences or put a tick by any you think are correct.

1 Doctor, I would be grateful if you can give me the news, good or bad.
....

2 Governments would work together to ensure that vaccines are available across the world.
....

3 Susanna is a brilliant chemist and I could recommend her to you entirely.
....

4 We haven't come to any definite conclusions, so we should do some more research.
....

5 It's possible that you can study medicine at university, but you need to work harder on your grades.
....

6 If you're feeling poorly, it can be a good idea to go to bed early.
....

VOCABULARY
HEALTH: PHRASAL VERBS AND EXPRESSIONS

1 Complete the table to form correct phrasal verbs related to health.

black	break	burn	come	fight (it)
freak	nod	pass (x2)	sleep (it)	

OUT	OFF	ROUND	ON	AWAY

2 Match the sentence halves.

1 Don't mention hospitals to me – I break
2 It's common to feel frequently burnt
3 I was on the sofa, nodding
4 If you're feeling poorly, go to bed and try to sleep it
5 He was really confused when he came
6 My friend completely freaked me
7 In the eighteenth century, people passed
8 My little sister is always passing

a out when she showed me her scar.
b round and saw the doctor looking down at him.
c out when you are revising non-stop for exams.
d off, when my cat jumped onto my chest.
e on all the germs she's picked up at nursery.
f out in a cold sweat just thinking about them.
g off – that's as good as any medicine.
h away at a younger age than they do today.

1 .... 3 .... 5 .... 7 ....
2 .... 4 .... 6 .... 8 ....

3 Complete the sentences with the verbs in the box in the correct form.

black	break	burn	came	fight
freak	nod	pass (x2)	sleep	

1 Denis looks really .... out. He's so pale and has dark circles under his eyes.
2 Tired after a long day at work, she was .... off in bed when her phone rang.
3 Have you ever .... out and woken up not knowing where you are? It's really scary.
4 People nowadays are much more careful not to .... on illnesses.
5 I was driving down the road when another car crashed into me. I .... round two days later in a hospital bed.
6 If you think you're ill, don't google what you think you've got – you'll .... out and convince yourself it's something awful.
7 Some people never seem to get ill, and if they do, they tend to .... it off really quickly.
8 Rafa woke up with a fever, so he's trying to .... it off in bed.
9 I've .... out in a sweat just thinking about my final exams next month. I'm so stressed and nervous about them!
10 I've just heard that Karen's grandfather has .... away. Shall we send some flowers?

4 Correct the health expressions 1–6 and match them to the definitions a–f.

1 on the fix ....
2 right in the rain ....
3 (all) as one piece ....
4 a cause to concern ....
5 didn't sleep any winks ....
6 over the weather ....

a not harmed
b getting better
c awake for most of the night
d poorly
e something to worry about
f completely healthy or well again

1 .... 3 .... 5 ....
2 .... 4 .... 6 ....

5 Complete the sentences with health expressions, using the words in the box.

cause	mend	piece	rain	weather	wink

1 Sandrine said she's ...., but she still doesn't feel 100% just yet.
2 If you're feeling poorly, have an early night and you'll feel .... in the morning.
3 My uncle's had a car accident. The car is in a bad way, but at least he's ....
4 I'm going to see the doctor later. Hopefully, this dark mark on my arm isn't ....
5 The neighbours had a crazy party all night. The noise was so deafening that I ....
6 George is going to stay home from school today. He's feeling ....

6 Complete the second sentence so that it means the same as the first sentence. Use a phrase from Exercises 4 and 5.

1 Toby said that he's feeling poorly, so he can't come over.
Toby said that he's ...., so he can't come over.
2 I was ill for a while, but I'm completely back to normal now.
I was ill for a while, but I'm .... now.
3 The doctor said my illness was nothing to worry about.
The doctor said my illness was ....
4 I was ill for a while, but I'm getting better now.
I was ill for a while, but I'm .... now.
5 Tina was unable to get any sleep last night – she was so excited.
Tina .... last night – she was so excited.
6 It looked bad when Rosa fell off her bike, but she didn't get injured, unbelievably.
It looked bad when Rosa fell off her bike, but she's ...., unbelievably.

7 Complete the sentences so that they are true for you.

1 ...., but it was no cause for concern in the end.
2 .... Thankfully, it was all in one piece.
3 There was once a night when I didn't sleep a wink because ....
4 It really freaked me out when ....

LISTENING

1 Why do you think this person might be wearing a virtual reality headset?

....

....

....

2 You are going to listen to a university student called Gabriel giving a talk about the uses of technology in a hospital. Look at question 1 in Exercise 6 and underline the key words.

3 Which of the following options could replace the word *different* in question 1 of Exercise 6?

A (a/the) range of
B other
C various
D all of the above

4 Which one of the options below does not make sense in the gap in question 1?

A standards
B fields
C studies

5 Read the first paragraph from the talk and complete question 1 in Exercise 6.

Hi, everyone. My name's Gabriel and I'm here to talk to you about a project I did related to my university studies in game design and virtual reality development. I've always been interested in how the many uses of technology in gaming are applied in other fields, so I was delighted to spend time at the Royal Hospital, looking at how my various studies might apply to the world of medical practice, where, of course, rigorous standards are in place.

6 Listen to Gabriel give his talk. For questions 1–8, complete the sentences with a word or short phrase.

03

1 Gabriel says he wanted to understand how different .... exploit the same technology that is used in games design.

2 Gabriel explains how a .... working at the hospital agreed to the proposal from his university department.

3 Gabriel says his aim was to investigate how the available .... could be improved for doctors.

4 Gabriel uses the phrase .... to explain the expertise required of surgeons.

5 Initially, Gabriel was unsure how reliable VR would be in the .... of a hospital.

6 When talking about wearing the VR headset at the hospital, Gabriel uses the word .... to describe his surroundings.

7 Gabriel says a practising surgeon showed him how to carry out some .... that junior doctors learn.

8 In Gabriel's opinion, ... offer vital opportunities to ensure that errors do not occur during surgery.

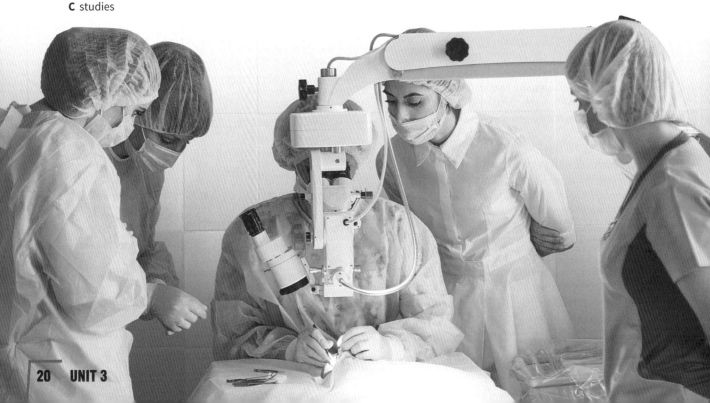

READING AND USE OF ENGLISH

1 Read the article in Exercise 4 quickly, ignoring the gaps. What is the writer's main idea?

2 Complete the sentences with the words in the box.

doubt ~~question~~ reason wonder

1 There's no *question* that your poor diet is making you feel ill.
2 It's no _____ that I'm so tired – I didn't sleep a wink last night.
3 There's no _____ to believe that you'll feel like this forever.
4 There's no _____ that smoking is bad for you.

3 Read the first sentence in the article in Exercise 4. Which of the words from the box in Exercise 2 is the correct answer to question (0) and why?

4 For questions 1–8, decide which answer (A, B, C or D) fits best in the gap.

Give yourself a break

We all know how hard people work and study these days, so it's no **(0)** _____ that stress-related illness has become a major **(1)** _____ for concern. The stereotypical image of the workaholic business executive can now be joined by that of the burnt-out student, putting in **(2)** _____ hours of study as they strive for the best qualifications possible.

Frankly, we have enough to worry about in the world without making ourselves unable to **(3)** _____ off illness through a lack of sleep and an excess of work or study. **(4)** _____ that, when people feel weak through overwork, it is **(5)** _____ that they will not be at their best, and they may end up burning their **(6)** _____ with a colleague, friend or family member. We cannot live in a world where it is common to **(7)** _____ with someone who we get on well with. This type of 'work at all costs' mentality must not be **(8)** _____ in stone.

5 Look at the two sentences, ignoring the gap. **Highlight** the words that are the same in both.
  A Despite what the doctor said, I'm still worried about dad's illness.
  B Dad's illness is still _____, despite what the doctor said.

6 Think about the words that remain. Which phrase that includes the word *cause* means 'to be worried about something'?

7 Look at question 1 in Exercise 8. Why is this answer incorrect?

Dad's illness is still <u>causing us concern</u>, despite what the doctor said.

8 For questions 1–6, complete the second sentence so that it has a similar meaning to the first sentence, using the word given. Do not change the word given. You must use between three and six words, including the word given.

1 Despite what the doctor said, we're still worried about dad's illness.
  CAUSE
  Dad's illness is still _____, despite what the doctor said.

2 My grandparents always brought me chocolate whenever they visited.
  WOULD
  Whenever my grandparents visited, _____ chocolate.

3 You will feel worse if you don't get out of bed soon.
  LONGER
  The _____ worse you will feel.

4 I don't think there's anything more we can do, so let's start again tomorrow.
  WALL
  I think we _____, so let's start again tomorrow.

5 Making great efforts preparing for parties isn't something Aria normally does.
  TOWN
  It's unlike Aria _____ preparations for parties.

6 Often, Isa gives people the impression that she's rude, but really she's just shy.
  ACROSS
  Isa often _____ rude, but really she's just shy.

0 A wonder	**B** reason	**C** question	**D** doubt
1 A matter	**B** origin	**C** factor	**D** cause
2 A immense	**B** countless	**C** massive	**D** constant
3 A push	**B** turn	**C** fight	**D** kick
4 A Considering	**B** In spite of	**C** Except	**D** Aside from
5 A positive	**B** significant	**C** inevitable	**D** definite
6 A towers	**B** bridges	**C** connections	**D** channels
7 A clash	**B** challenge	**C** object	**D** oppose
8 A left	**B** set	**C** kept	**D** put

VOCABULARY AND READING
MAKING DECISIONS

1 Read the blog post below and choose the correct options.

→ Following the signs ←

On reaching a crossroads in life, at a point when you are ⁰ *considering / holding / reflecting* your options, it may seem impossible to ¹ *make on / make up / make out* your mind about which path to follow, and you may find yourself becoming stressed. This is particularly common in people who are always in two ² *ideas / minds / thoughts* about anything they do. This type of uncertainty can lead to too much time spent on ³ *considering / weighing / holding* up the pros and cons, so to avoid this happening, the next logical step should be ⁴ *finding / seeking / discovering* advice from someone you trust. Take time to think ⁵ *across / past / through* your options together, and you may find that two or more heads are better than one. It is vital to bear in mind that each route will offer something unexpectedly positive, however unsure ⁶ *on / for / about* change you might feel. Choices can be seen as opportunities for growth.

2 Use the capitalised initials in bold to form the correct phrase in each sentence.

0 My parents are expecting me to go to university straight after college. But going on a gap year looks so interesting. I'm really **ITM** about what's best. _in two minds_

1 We were hoping to tell you today whether or not you've got the job, but I'm afraid we've not quite **CTAD** yet.

2 When Mario inherited a large sum of money, he started **WUTPAC** of buying a new car.

3 Before we start this project, I think we should all get together to **B** some **I**.

4 For our wedding next year, we know exactly which guests we want to invite, but we're still **IDA** which venue to hire.

5 Your grades were great in English and history, but not so good in science and maths. Maybe it's time to **R** your options, as studying architecture may not be for you.

6 As people get older, they tend to take more time to **TT** their options when important life decisions come along.

7 It's perfectly natural to **BUA** what to do next when you finish your education – there are some big decisions to make.

8 Katya doesn't know anyone in Barcelona, so she's still **UA** whether to take that internship she was offered there.

3 Complete the sentences so that they are true for you.

1 The last time I decided to seek advice was when

2 I often find that brainstorming ideas is

3 Earlier this week, I was in two minds about

4 In the future, I may need to reconsider

5 I find it easier to make up my mind when

4 Read the introduction to the reviews on the opposite page. Think of three reasons why the documentary series might be interesting to watch and three reasons why it might not appeal to you.

5 Read the reviews on the opposite page quickly. Which reviewer enjoyed the series the most?

6 For questions 1–4, choose from the reviews (A–D). The reviews may be chosen more than once.

Which review

1 has a different opinion to the others about the structure of the series?

2 shares D's view of how successfully the presenter of the series did their job?

3 agrees with A about the group of people who the series is most likely to appeal to?

4 disagrees with C about the importance to wider society of a series such as *Next Steps*?

7 Match the highlighted words and phrases in the article to the meanings.

1 completely

2 a change in position or direction

3 talk honestly about something personal to someone else

4 send out a programme on television, radio or other media

5 things that are successful, or achieved after a lot of work or effort

NEXT STEPS

A   *Next Steps* allows us to dip into the lives of three likeable young people, taking a fascinating look at how adolescents become young adults in today's world. The first show focuses on their struggles, while the second hour deals only with their ambitions and accomplishments. It is a stylish split that works perfectly, ending on a feeling of optimism in which they all have clear ideas about their 'next steps'. Though presenter Carrie Clarke sometimes seems disconnected from the subject matter, when a documentary is made this well, it has the potential to be a powerful force for good, informing us about what is going on in other people's lives . That said, while I couldn't stop watching for a moment, my teenage daughters were frankly unimpressed, so perhaps it was older viewers like me who were meant to enjoy it most.

B   These days, TV documentaries very rarely have a lasting effect on our attitudes and beliefs (nor should they) and so I did not go into the social documentary *Next Steps* with enormously high expectations. The lows of the adolescents' lives are dealt with in the opening episode, before moving onto the highs in the second, and this clearly made sense from the director's perspective as they could finish on a convenient happy ending. But life at this age can be messy, so it ultimately seemed a strange way to document their shift towards early adulthood. Considering that my own journey happened over ten years ago now, perhaps I wasn't the best person to assess how successfully the series truly represented all teenagers' lives. Nevertheless, younger people who are at a similar point of choosing their specific path to follow should be able to find much to relate to.

C   Now more than ever, we need TV programmes that can bring together people from all social backgrounds to share their experiences, generating greater understanding in the outside world. *Next Steps* managed to do this commendably well. The presenter deserves much credit, as all three of the subjects opened up to her without any sense of reservation or embarrassment. Viewers could easily relate to their problems and concerns, and I found myself hoping that the stars of the show have since found life to be stimulating and rewarding. I did feel that the series could have made even more of an impact on people if it hadn't been simply divided into two distinct episodes – negative experiences followed by positive ones – but it was certainly enjoyable enough for me to recommend to friends and family.

D   There is not a huge amount new in terms of the concept of *Next Steps*. Throughout the years, there has been no shortage of documentaries that focus on an element of society and broadcast it to the public. I found it an enjoyable series, despite not being entirely convinced by the approach – dark in episode one, light in episode two – as it felt a little too simplistic and not entirely representative of how life is actually lived. Certainly, it is a struggle to find fault with Carrie Clarke as presenter, who allowed the teenagers to develop their stories in a compassionate way. As someone who has recently become a young adult, I could wholly empathise with much of what they were going through, like applying for jobs which they were never going to be offered, or trying (and failing) to get into their chosen university. Yet, however familiar it felt to me, I couldn't help but think that the series would be of most interest to parents of teenagers, rather than the age group being shown on screen (and, presumably, the target audience).

GRAMMAR
MODALS IN THE PAST

1 Choose the correct options.

1 Finally, after ten minutes of looking through my bags, I *could / was able to* find my passport.

2 Christian *couldn't have failed / didn't need to fail* his science test – he's almost as clever as the teacher.

3 Just before my eighteenth birthday, my parents told me I *could / was able to* start taking driving lessons.

4 My grandmother had ten children, so she *should have / must have* been constantly exhausted.

5 In the end, the exam was much easier than we had expected, so we *needn't have worried / mustn't have worried*.

6 I *had to / was allowed to* open my own bank account before I could go to university.

7 You *ought to / needed to* have told me you were thinking of changing schools.

8 Often, during the school holidays, I *was allowed to go / should have gone* to work with my dad.

2 Write the modal verbs from Exercise 1 in the table below.

Ability	
Permission	
Obligation/Lack of obligation	
Advice	
Speculation/Deduction	

3 Put the words in italics in the correct order.

1 *shouldn't been have I* so unfair to you. I'm sorry for what I said.

2 *able paper to exam was the complete he* in under an hour.

3 *have it you can't easy been for*, growing up with a brother like Tino.

4 *must you that playing game been have* for at least eight hours yesterday.

4 Tick the correct sentence in each pair.

1 **A** My teachers very patiently explained that they mustn't have put me in a class on my own.
B My teachers very patiently explained that they weren't able to put me in a class on my own.

2 **A** We should be completely happy with that – it couldn't have gone any better.
B We should be completely happy with that – it mustn't have gone any better.

3 **A** In the end, we couldn't have brought our towels on holiday as there were plenty at the hotel.
B In the end, we needn't have brought our towels on holiday as there were plenty at the hotel.

4 **A** I can't wait until next week for your essay – you really ought to have finished by now.
B I can't wait until next week for your essay – you really needn't have finished by now.

5 Rewrite these sentences so that they refer to the past.

1 We needn't push ourselves so hard to make a decision.
We _____ pushed ourselves so hard to make a decision.

2 You mustn't keep letting him borrow your homework.
I wasn't _____ borrow my homework.

3 You should tell me if you're feeling worried about going to university.
You _____ feeling worried about going to university.

4 The rules clearly state that students must be on time for all lectures.
The rules clearly stated _____ for all lectures.

6 Correct the mistakes in the sentences or put a tick by any you think are correct.

1 Have you seen Alexis' amazing new car? It should cost a fortune. _____

2 The weather wasn't great on our holiday, so I think it would be better to go in summer.
_____

3 Angelo's bag is there, so he can't have gone home yet. _____

4 Juan had to email the careers advisor three times before she would have seen him.

5 I don't understand this question, mum. I must have asked the teacher for help in class.
_____

7 Complete the second sentence so that it has a similar meaning to the first sentence, using the word given. Do not change the word given. You must use between three and six words, including the word given.

1 I'm almost certain I forgot to bring my phone charger with me from Sara's house.   **BEHIND**
I think I must _____ at Sara's house.

2 I was so busy last week that watching that new TV show was impossible.   **ABLE**
I _____ that new TV show because I was so busy last week.

3 We went through a lot of unnecessary worry about what was going to happen.   **MUCH**
We needn't _____ about what was going to happen.

4 There was no point in upsetting your parents like that.   **OUGHT**
You _____ your parents like that.

5 Peter was in trouble with his parents, who said he couldn't see his friends.   **ALLOWED**
Because he was in trouble with his parents, Peter _____ up with his friends.

6 I think I saw Luis in town earlier, but perhaps it was his brother.   **BEEN**
I think I saw Luis in town earlier, although _____ his brother.

VOCABULARY
LIFE EVENTS: VERB AND NOUN COLLOCATIONS

1 Choose the correct options. In some sentences, more than one option is possible.

1 After a huge amount of thought, I've decided to *accept / choose* a place at the University of Valencia.

2 These days, graduates have to *apply for / take* so many jobs before they even get an interview.

3 Going abroad to study is such a huge *walk / step* – I hope you're ready for it.

4 I've just heard from my cousin. He's been *sent / offered* a place at all five of his university choices.

5 It's so important in life to *choose / follow* a path you think you'll be happy with.

6 Simon's a lot more optimistic about the future now that he's *done / got* an apprenticeship at a construction company.

7 It's never easy to *get / graduate* into university when your grades are lower than your teachers had predicted.

8 Once I *get / graduate* from university, I'm going to go on a very long holiday.

9 In most of Europe, people are only allowed to leave *school / university* when they are 18.

10 It may not be the case everywhere, but in my school the teachers *sit / set* exams for the students.

11 If your results are not what you are hoping for, you can always *resit / fail* your exams next year.

12 I've decided to *get / take* a gap year before I go to university.

2 Which other collocations can you use to talk about life events?

1 apply for
   an apprenticeship
2 do _____
3 get _____
4 leave _____
5 take _____

3 Which other verbs form collocations with the noun *(an) exam*?

_____

4 Complete the sentences with the correct option.

1 My cousin has finally _____ a place at the University of Cambridge – I don't know what took her so long.
  A applied   **B** accepted   **C** taken

2 There's always the option of _____ a gap year if your exam results aren't what you need.
  A taking   **B** sitting   **C** passing

3 Stefan is hoping to get into _____ a year early. He's so clever.
  A school   **B** an apprenticeship   **C** university

4 Starting from next week, I'm doing a three-month _____ in journalism.
  A exam   **B** course   **C** path

5 Depending on how my results go, I may have to _____ the exam in July.
  A have   **B** set   **C** resit

5 Complete the email using the collocations from Exercises 1–4.

Hi Emily,

Thanks for getting in touch. I'll try and give you the best advice I can.

Universities are generally impressed with students who have other interests outside of school or college, so it might be worth [0] *doing a course* in something you're interested in to improve your chances when you [1] _____ at university.

If your results come and you find that you haven't [2] _____, it would be disappointing, but you'd still have options. Perhaps speak to your teachers and ask if you can [3] _____ your exams at a later time. This way you can study more, so you're better prepared. And, for students who are less strong in their school or college subjects, it may be a good idea for them to [4] _____, as they get to learn directly from professionals as they train. But I don't think you need to worry about [5] _____ your _____, as you always seem to get the top grades when I speak to your mum.

I'm so glad to see that you're already thinking about your future and trying to choose a [6] _____ to follow when you leave college next year. Remember, you don't have to decide immediately. So many young people now [7] _____ to travel, work or both. They also use this time to consider their options about the future. If you go abroad, this may also get your mum used to not having you around, in preparation for when you [8] _____ and go to university.

Speak soon,

Uncle David

ADJECTIVE AND NOUN COLLOCATIONS

6 Choose the correct options. In some sentences, more than one option is possible.

1 I left school when I was 16 to start my own business. It was a *strong / big / vital* decision at the time, but I've never regretted it.

2 We're going to a careers advisor to discuss our plans for the long term and for the *immediate / major / mixed* future.

3 My teachers at secondary school had such a *strong / immediate / vital* influence on me that, 50 years later, I still remember them.

4 There have been some *big / major / strong* changes in education over the past few years, particularly the move to online learning.

5 A conscientious attitude and an enquiring mind play *vital / major / strong* roles in academic success.

6 In her literature essay, Esme displayed a *clear / mixed / strong* understanding of the Romantic poets.

7 When choosing a university, location is often the *deciding / vital / major* factor for many students.

WRITING
AN ESSAY

» SEE *PREPARE TO WRITE* BOX, STUDENT'S BOOK PAGE 33

1 Make a list of the options a student needs to consider after finishing a university degree.

....

....

....

2 Read the question. Do any of your ideas from Exercise 1 apply to the *Factors to consider*?

> Your class has been discussing the options available to people who are choosing which path to follow after their university degrees.
>
> **Factors to consider:**
> * amount of personal debt
> * desire to remain in education
> * level of professional ambition
>
> **Some opinions expressed in the discussion:**
> 'If you owe thousands on a student loan, you have to get a job and start paying it back immediately.'
> 'Learning is not always something that you can turn off the moment you gain a qualification.'
> 'Some people are entirely focused on becoming a success in the working world.'

3 Look at the student's notes (0–5) and decide which of the factors (A–C) they most likely relate to.

A Amount of personal debt
B Desire to remain in education
C Level of professional ambition

0 Gain knowledge/enjoyment from studies	BUT	Life in work = attractive
1 Personal/Social growth at uni	BUT	need to be free from loans
2 Staying at uni = attractive	BUT	working world more appealing
3 Postgraduate study still very popular	BUT	not beneficial for 'real world'
4 Few career opportunities in higher education	BUT	stimulating/supportive environment
5 New graduates optimistic about future	BUT	debts huge and may influence choice of job

0 _C_   **1** ....   **2** ....   **3** ....   **4** ....   **5** ....

4 Read the essay written in response to Exercise 2. Which two factors has the student chosen to talk about?

At the end of a degree course, graduates are faced with the decision of what to do next in their lives. Two influential factors are whether or not to stay in education and the levels of personal debt they have built up.

Firstly, ¹ although graduates may have a lot of money in student loans to repay, but the move into the world of work can often seem difficult to manage. Often, they have spent three years or more in a close academic community, where the focus is purely on learning and discovering new theories and ideas. It is natural that they might feel keen to explore these further. Additionally, ² staying on in education is often said to lead to a lack of engagement in the 'real world', while postgraduate courses are still hugely in demand, and can lead to better employment opportunities in the future.

On the other hand, ³ despite of the personal and social growth that students experience, huge numbers of them are desperate to live a life free from loan repayments. In this way, paying back huge amounts of money is the primary factor in deciding what their next step should be. ⁴ In spite of feel optimistic about their futures, it is extremely difficult for new graduates to ignore the huge debts they have built up, and they know that it will take years, even decades, to pay it all back. It is no wonder, then, that they want to start earning a salary as soon as possible.

In my opinion, any graduate's decision is most likely to be influenced by their need to pay back the debts they owe which, as I have mentioned, are often considerable.

5 Make corrections to the underlined parts of the essay.

6 Rewrite the sentences using the words in brackets.

0 A student may enjoy studying their degree course, but it is not necessarily relevant to their future career. (Although)
Although a student may enjoy studying their degree course, it is not necessarily relevant to their future career.

1 A degree is often considered essential, but earning a good living is possible without one. (Despite)

2 Many parents expect their children to start work, but remaining in education may be the best possible option. (However)

3 Some people greatly enjoy their studies at university, but they thrive when they enter the working world. (While)

4 It's a great expense, but a degree still opens up a huge number of opportunities. (In spite of)

5 Many people are keen to continue their studies. Others cannot wait to leave university and start work. (In contrast)

6 Postgraduate courses are still hugely in demand, but they may not be the best option for people who are keen to test themselves in the 'real world'. (nevertheless)

7 Choose the correct options.

1 People start a degree course with a *major / clear* understanding that, when they leave, they will owe a huge amount of money.
2 It is common to have *mixed / deciding* feelings when the time comes to graduate from university.
3 Motivation plays a(n) *vital / immediate* role in how far someone succeeds in their professional career.
4 Often, new graduates have already made *clear / major* changes to their lives – when they first left home to study at university, for example.
5 When considering their next move, the *vital / deciding* factor for most graduates is how much debt they need to pay off.
6 After graduation, it is natural to feel worried about your *mixed / immediate* future, especially after spending time in a close academic community.

8 Read this section from another student's answer to the essay question in Exercise 2. Complete the text with two of the corrected sentences from Exercise 7.

> On the other hand, staying in full-time education is not always possible.
> 1
> .
>
> Students whose parents are not rich have to support themselves in their studies, and they can often only do this by taking on loans. It is true that
> 2
> .
>
> Yet the figure they need to repay is often much higher than they expected, and their only motivation when they leave is to clear this debt as soon as possible.

9 Read the essay question. Choose the two points you are going to focus on and make notes.

> Your class has been discussing the importance of asking for advice when making important decisions in life and which sources young people should use to get this advice. You have made the notes below:
>
> **Which sources are most likely to provide young people with the best advice for important life decisions?**
> • friends/family
> • internet websites
> • teachers/lecturers
>
> > **Some opinions expressed in the discussion:**
> > 'Your friends and family know you better than anyone and know what's best for you.'
> > 'On the internet, you can easily find advice from thousands of highly-qualified people.'
> > 'Teachers and educators can give advice both from a professional and personal point of view.'

10 Write an essay discussing two of the sources in your notes. You should explain which source is more important for offering advice, giving reasons for your opinion. Write your essay in 220–260 words.

VOCABULARY AND READING
TECHNOLOGY AND PROGRESS

1 Complete the words with the missing vowels.

0 d e v e l o pm e nt
1 br___kthr___gh
2 r___d___c___l
3 m___rk___t
4 ___bs___l___t
5 c___tt___ng___dg
6 pr___t___typ___
7 dr___wb___ck
8 l___nch
9 ___dv___nc___s
10 tr___gg___r

2 Match the definitions to the words from Exercise 1.

1 cause something to start ___
2 causing or being an example of great change ___
3 improvements or developments in something ___
4 a disadvantage or the negative part of a situation ___
5 begin something such as a plan or introduce something new such as a product ___
6 the most modern stage of development in a particular type of work or activity ___
7 make goods available to buyers in a planned way that encourages people to buy more of them ___
8 an important discovery or event that helps to improve a situation or provide an answer to a problem ___
9 not in use any more, having been replaced by something newer and better or more fashionable ___
10 the first example of something, such as a machine or other industrial product, from which all later forms are developed ___

3 Choose the correct options.

1 We have made huge technological *advances / drawbacks* in the field of medicine recently.
2 There were several *breakthroughs / drawbacks* of only selling their product online. For example, the customer could not see or feel the product.
3 Video tapes became *obsolete / radical* during the 2000s – nobody uses them anymore.
4 The better a product is, the easier it is to *trigger / market*.
5 My business uses *cutting edge / prototype* technology to build its latest products.
6 Scientists have announced that they have made an astonishing *breakthrough / launch* in driverless technology.
7 Our home-study software has *triggered / launched* the development of new approaches to education.
8 There are a number of *prototype / radical* differences between gaming technology today compared to twenty years ago.
9 Aidan's company is going to *launch / radical* its new product at the global conference next month.
10 Many of the great *innovations / drawbacks* over the past few centuries have begun as a simple idea.

4 Which invention do you think has had the most influence on our lives today? Why?

....

....

5 For questions 1–3, read the options A–C. Which of the pictures do you think each set of options refers to?

 arch
 assembly line

 printing press

1 ___
A It was originally invented by the Romans. ___
B It contributed to increased safety in Roman communities. ___
C It was part of every Roman building used for official business. ___

2 ___
A It is an essential part of modern manufacturing. ___
B It has had an entirely positive impact on society. ___
C It helped to improve working conditions for staff. ___

3 ___
A It was occasionally used by people of the highest status to print their work. ___
B It was created with the aim of making its inventor famous. ___
C It was used by public officials to connect with their community. ___

6 Read the three texts on the opposite page quickly to check your ideas.

7 Read the texts again. Are the statements in Exercise 5 *T* (True), *F* (False) or *NM* (Not Mentioned)?

8 Match the highlighted words in the article to the meanings.

1 very great, dominant ___
2 machines, or pieces of equipment (especially electricals one) that are used at home ___
3 extremely important because other things depend on it ___
4 the ability to read and write ___
5 having an appearance that looks important or causes admiration ___

Great inventions

1

Over two thousand years ago, when the ancient Romans were building city after city, they were able to make advances in the field of construction and, as a result, the strength of their civilisation. This came with the help of something which we now see everywhere – the arch. The Romans' arch design consisted of a curved top on two supports, which was able to hold considerable weight. There had been prototypes of the arch over previous centuries, developed by other groups, but these were far less able to carry huge loads in the same way (mainly due to having a horizontal top, rather than a curved one).

And this is why the arch is one of the most important innovations in human history. Arches allowed the Romans to build aqueducts – huge, imposing structures that were able to support and carry enormous volumes of water long distances, directing a constant supply of fresh water from mountains or hills to new towns and villages. The arch also allowed the Romans to build stronger and larger bridges that crossed valleys and rivers. This, along with the increased availability of fresh water, helped the Romans expand their territory and conquer new lands. The arch's design also helped them strengthen their city walls, so they were more capable of defending this territory.

The arch wasn't only used to expand the empire. It was also used in the construction of *basilicas* – public buildings (with a curved roof) which hosted meetings and performances.

The arch is ultimately responsible for your safety, your towns and cities, your home and your entertainment venues. Oh, and your water supply. So, everything, really.

2

By 1913, the automobile had been in existence for around thirty years. However, they were still enormously expensive at this point, and the majority of citizens could not afford to buy one. This was partly due to the fact that it would take a group of workers over half a day just to build one car.

But this was the year that Henry Ford created the moving assembly line and, in doing so, triggered great changes in vehicle production. Designed to allow for the workers, machines and parts to be organised in sequence, the speed of production was accelerated. With this system in place, it took only 90 minutes to put together a car, meaning that the price to the consumer fell dramatically and a population would soon become mobilised.

This formed a pivotal moment in history as the assembly line spread across the world and became the driving force of mass production. Suddenly, large-scale production processes meant that people could afford what they had never been able to before, and the age of the consumer was born. Indeed, such a huge amount of what we buy and consume is still sent through this automated process, from household appliances and electronic goods to plastic bowls of microwaveable food. The assembly line as a source of overwhelming good is not a view that everybody shares, but there can be little doubt that Henry Ford's innovation is a crucial part of our society today.

3

It would be wonderful to think that Johan Gutenberg created the printing press with the noble aim of bringing literacy to as many people as possible, but this wasn't necessarily the case. The fact is, he had understood how lucrative it could be to mass-produce a certain product, and his development of the 'movable type machine' – the printing press – provided him with exactly the money-making opportunity he was looking for.

Up until that point, books had been produced entirely by hand and were hugely expensive – a sign of wealth and status. The elite classes, instead of embracing this radical new technology, looked down on what was being created – unsatisfactory imitations of their precious, hand-written texts. But the printing press began a revolution that threatened their wealth and status by allowing information to be read by huge numbers of people.

Print became the medium of the lower classes. It enabled them to read widely, develop their ideas and educate themselves. Academics were able to publish their theories and politicians could engage with the community through the distribution of booklets. Perhaps most importantly of all, since people wanted to read texts in their own regional languages, it was the beginning of the end for Latin as the language of all written communication and the start of a new approach to learning and understanding.

GRAMMAR
THE FUTURE

1 **Choose the correct options.**

1 The government hopes that pollution levels *will be declining / will have declined* by 20% by the end of the year.

2 In the future, more people *will be working / will have been working* from home than in offices.

3 By the year 2050, companies *will be offering / will have been offering* tourist flights into space.

4 On 25th March, I'*ll be working / 'll have been working* here for five years.

5 The best time to call me is at 10 pm because *I'll have finished / I'll finish* my homework at that point.

6 Don't look sad – *we'll meet up / we'll have met up* again very soon.

7 I've sent you a link to a great blog I've been reading. I'm sure *you'll find / you'll be finding* it interesting.

8 We *were going / will be going* to go for dinner this evening, but decided not to in the end.

9 My first driving lesson went really well. I had no idea it *would / will* be as much fun as that.

10 Can I call you back later? *I'll be having / I'm about to have* lunch.

2 **Complete the sentences using the words in brackets in present simple or present continuous form. In some sentences, both are correct.**

1 I .... (get) the food for the party tomorrow. You need to buy the drinks.

2 After the party ...., (finish) we can get a taxi back home.

3 The bus is always late, so we .... (walk) to school tomorrow.

4 I think the science fair you were telling me about .... (start) at the weekend.

5 When we .... (receive) the results, we'll be able to see if the experiment has worked.

6 We don't know the exact travel plan, but we do know we .... (end) the year in Tbilisi.

7 Julia .... (move) to Canada to complete her Masters in engineering.

8 I .... (leave) no later than 6 am tomorrow – the traffic can get really bad in the morning.

3 **Choose the best option in these conversations.**

1 **A:** Shall I phone you at half past three?
B: *I'll be driving / I'll have driven* to my parent's house then, so maybe four is better.

2 **A:** It's amazing how much time flies, isn't it?
B: It really is! This time next month, *we'll be knowing / we'll have known* each other for thirty years.

3 **A:** What are your plans for this evening?
B: Well, *I was going to / I'm going to* start my project in the garden. Looking at the weather, though, I might leave it until tomorrow.

4 **A:** I can't help you with the shopping, mum. Sorry, but I've got too much homework.
B: OK, *I'll ask / I'm asking* your sister then.

5 **A:** Have you decided on where you're living during your first year at university?
B: *I'm going to live / I'll have lived* in the university accommodation for the first year, but hopefully somewhere else after that.

4 **Complete the sentences with the correct option. In some sentences, more than one option is possible.**

1 Over the next year, the quality of television shows .... even further.
A is about to improve **B** will improve **C** would improve

2 Hopefully, we .... each other again next month.
A see **B** 're going to see **C** 'll see

3 After I .... my exam results, there might be tears of joy or despair.
A get **B** 'll get **C** 'm going to get

4 I .... take the bike to your house, but now it's raining. I think the car is a better option.
A was going to **B** was about to **C** will

5 Can you call back in about an hour? We .... sit down for dinner.
A 'll **B** 're about to **C** 're going to

6 That documentary was really interesting. I think I .... watch it again at the weekend.
A 'm about to **B** 'm going to **C** 'll

7 Lectures .... at exactly 9 am, so please make every effort to be on time.
A begin **B** will begin **C** would begin

8 Why don't we take our telescopes up into the hills tonight and look at the stars? I ....
A 'll drive **B** 'm going to drive **C** drive

5 **Correct the mistakes in the sentences or put a tick by any you think are correct.**

1 I'm sure you'll find the room extremely comfortable.
....

2 After you've checked out, follow the signs which lead to the station. ....

3 I hope I feel more confident by the time we'll be studying at university. ....

4 I'm convinced that we're able to raise enough money to renovate the school gym. ....

5 She'll have finished her course soon, so we'll be able to do more stuff together. ....

6 Apparently, the printer has broken. I really hope it will work tomorrow.

7 This time next week, we'll be having staff training.
....

8 Once you will have received your luggage, go down the stairs. ....

VOCABULARY
ADJECTIVES AND DEPENDENT PREPOSITIONS

1 Complete the sentences with the correct option.

1 Many people feel _____ towards new technology, especially when they don't understand it.
A vulnerable   B toxic   C hostile

2 Batteries contain chemicals that are extremely _____ to humans.
A notorious   B hostile   C toxic

3 Computers from five years ago are greatly _____ to the ones you can buy today.
A inferior   B notorious   C vulnerable

4 It isn't _____ for students to comment on how teachers look.
A apparent   B appropriate   C conscious

5 In the 1990s, computers were _____ for crashing before you could save your work.
A notorious   B vulnerable   C hostile

6 It was _____ to Bill Gates that he was going to start a revolution in computers.
A appropriate   B conscious   C apparent

7 Unless you have adequate protection, all of your online accounts are _____ to hackers.
A addicted   B vulnerable   C conscious

8 When conducting research, it is important to be _____ of how unsafe some sites are.
A conscious   B apparent   C appropriate

2 Complete the sentences with the answers from Exercise 1 and the correct preposition.

1 I'm extremely _____ the fact that time is running out, so let's hurry up and try to finish.

2 It's surprising how many people feel _____ the idea of buying an electric car.

3 Certain plants are _____ pets and should not be planted in the garden.

4 We have recently been reminded of how _____ new viruses people are.

5 It is a fantastic film, but it's probably not _____ younger children.

6 When I showed Laura my homework, all of my mistakes were immediately _____ her.

PHRASAL VERBS

3 Match the words in the box to the definitions.

> catch on   cater for   check out   do away with
> lie ahead   look upon as   run on   rush into

1 be in the future _____
2 try, look at, examine _____
3 become fashionable or popular _____
4 use a particular type of energy to work _____
5 remove completely _____
6 provide what is wanted or needed by someone or something _____
7 consider or think of someone or something in a particular way _____
8 start doing something without having decided if it is the right thing to do or considered how to do it
_____

4 Complete the sentences with the phrasal verbs from Exercise 3.

1 A growing number of cars _____ electricity these days.

2 I got a Gameplay console for my birthday. Come over at the weekend and _____ it _____.

3 When I was younger, I _____ my studies _____ a huge inconvenience.

4 Our long-term goal must be to _____ fossil fuels completely.

5 There are a number of challenges that _____ for the entertainment industry, such as the fact that people don't go to the cinema regularly anymore.

6 Many games companies don't seem to _____ people over the age of thirty.

7 I wonder if electric cars will ever _____ completely. Many people are still reluctant to use them.

8 You've got so many options available to choose from, so take your time and don't _____ anything.

☑ 5 For questions 1–8, read the text and think of the word which best fits each gap. Use only one word in each gap.

What is *planned obsolescence*?

Have you suddenly become aware **(0)** _of_ not being able to watch an entire movie on your laptop without your battery needing a recharge? Is it apparent **(1)** _____ you that, over time, the battery dies more quickly than it used to? Maybe you could find a laptop than runs **(2)** _____ solar power …

The truth is, many technology companies have done **(3)** _____ with the commitment to long-term reliability. *Planned obsolescence* ensures that a product only works for a limited time before needing to be replaced. This might explain why many people argue that products today are inferior **(4)** _____ the ones of the past – as they are built to fail. Some companies are utterly notorious **(5)** _____ doing this. They are constantly thinking about what lies **(6)** _____ and working on the updated model you will need to buy when your phone dies.

Planned obsolescence has come to be looked **(7)** _____ as entirely acceptable to us modern consumers. We are all conscious **(8)** _____ 'needing' to get the latest model of any electronic goods that we own.

6 Complete the sentences with *of*, *for* or *to*.

0 I completely understand why people are suspicious _of_ saving all their passwords on their devices.

1 These days, there's no point being resistant _____ the advances of technological development.

2 Now that I've finished university, I'm eager _____ the next stage of my life to begin.

3 Contrary _____ popular belief, not all teenagers are obsessed with their smart phones.

4 This game contains some scenes of violence, so is unsuitable _____ children.

5 It's unhealthy to feel envious _____ people who have thousands of followers online.

6 It's typical _____ Raul to turn up with the new iPhone on the day it's launched.

LISTENING

1 **What do you think are the main challenges when designing a new app? Make a list.**

_____

_____

 2 **You are going to listen to an interview with two people who have launched an app design company. Listen to the first part of the interview and answer the question below in your own words.**

What does Andrew believe is the main appeal of apps?

_____

 3 **Listen to the first part of the interview again. Read the question. Choose the correct option and compare it with your answer in Exercise 2.**

1 Andrew believes that the main appeal of apps is that
   A they encourage people to be more sociable.
   B they provide access to commercial services.
   C they offer a range of entertainment sources.
   D they allow people more control over their lives.

4 **Read the transcript of what Andrew said. Underline the words that gave you the answer to Exercise 3 and put a cross next to the sections which refer to the other options.**

> Well, look at how different life has become over the past decade. With apps, we can find any product we need and businesses can offer their services to millions of potential clients, so there's a clear commercial benefit for many, many people. And even if you don't use apps for that type of thing, there's little else in life that isn't covered by an app. I think everyone completely appreciates how they help us to manage our activities and interests according to our own preferences, whether you're an extrovert who can't keep off social media, or the quieter type who prefers watching movies on their smart phone.

 5 **Listen to the rest of the interview. For questions 2–6, choose the answer (A, B, C or D) which fits best according to what you hear.**

2 In Andrew's opinion, what is most important about the initial stages of app design?
   A to investigate how much existing competition there is
   B to spend time developing the relevant technical skills
   C to have confidence in how strong the initial idea is
   D to approach potential clients to ask for their feedback

3 Andrew talks about their first app in order to illustrate
   A the advantages of being able to multitask.
   B how people can frequently deceive themselves.
   C the need to be convincing to potential customers.
   D how negative experiences can lead to opportunity.

4 Lydia says that when she took the online course, she was
   A pleased to be able to impress a family member.
   B embarrassed at how difficult she found it.
   C surprised by how much there was to learn.
   D unsure about whether she had made the right choice.

5 Lydia explains that the aspect of the job she enjoys is
   A supporting clients in their commercial growth.
   B teaching demanding clients about app development.
   C persuading clients to make more suitable choices.
   D working with clients who already have a design in mind.

6 When talking about the benefits of working in the technology industry, Andrew and Lydia disagree about
   A the advantage of being the age they are.
   B the unpredictability of the working day.
   C the lack of interference from other people.
   D the improvements made by continual adaptation.

6 **Listen again to a section of the interview and complete the paragraph with the words or phrases you hear.**

> All you need initially is a concept. Good ideas do form the ¹ _____ of your future success, but even so, it's important not to get carried away and rush into ² _____ hours to coding and developing an app that isn't going to catch on. Your ³ _____ focus early on should always be research. You don't want to end up wasting your time, so find out whether or not similar products are already on the market. As long as you can see a ⁴ _____, at that point you can go ahead and start figuring out whether other people are going to download and use it as much as you hope they will.

7 **Match the definitions to the answers in Exercise 6.**

1 main, most important _____
2 giving your time and effort completely to something you believe in _____
3 an opportunity for a product or service that does not already exist _____
4 the most important facts or ideas from which something is developed _____

READING AND USE OF ENGLISH

1 Match the sentence halves.

1 I had trouble sleeping last night. I think I finally managed to **drop**
2 The new *Fast Cars* movie is so bad. It was so boring that I **fell**
3 During the holidays, I **go to**
4 I was so tired after I did the 10 km run that I **crashed**

a **asleep** half-way through!
b **off** at about 4 am.
c **out** on the sofa as soon as I got home.
d **sleep** a lot later than I do during term time.

1 .... 2 .... 3 .... 4 ....

2 What connects all of the phrases in bold above?

....

3 Complete the sentences with the words in the box.

careful   carefree   careless   caring

1 I remember those .... days when I was a child.
2 You might lose all the data on your device if you're not ....
3 It was really .... of him to leave his computer unlocked.
4 She can come across as insensitive sometimes, but deep down she's really ....

4 Now look at question (2) in Exercise 5. Which answer do you think is correct? ....

5 Read the text below and decide which answer (A, B, C or D) best fits each gap.

A **LUCKY** ESCAPE

One day last week, I was on a bus and I must have **(0)** *dropped* off because I suddenly realised we'd reached a bus stop that was **(1)** .... past mine. Instinctively, I jumped up and ran out, forgetting to pick up my bag with my laptop inside. I'd never usually do anything so **(2)** ...., but I'd barely slept a **(3)** .... the night before and my mind was still foggy.

As the bus pulled away, I realised with horror what I'd done and started shouting at the driver. He can't have noticed me because the bus just accelerated away. I considered my **(4)** .... briefly, before it suddenly became **(5)** .... what I should do: run to try to catch up with the bus. Having **(6)** .... into a serious sweat, I did eventually catch up three stops later and ran through the open door as passengers got off. Amazingly, someone had handed my bag in to the driver, and the laptop was inside it, all in one **(7)** .... It just goes to show people are often a lot more **(8)** .... than you might think.

0 (A) dropped	B fell	C went	D crashed
1 A much	B quite	C well	D so
2 A caring	B careful	C carefree	D careless
3 A flash	B blink	C wink	D tick
4 A selections	B options	C ideas	D needs
5 A apparent	B explicit	C visible	D prominent
6 A strained	B worked	C shattered	D broken
7 A piece	B part	C size	D item
8 A valid	B trustworthy	C credible	D faithful

6 For question 1, complete the second sentence so that it has a similar meaning to the first sentence, using one of the options A–C.

1 Parents should be in charge of limiting their children's screen time.
HAVE
Parents .... their children's screen time.

 A who are responsible, have a limit for
 B have a responsibly to limit
 C have a responsibility to limit

7 Why are the other options incorrect?

....
....
....

8 For questions 2–6, complete the second sentence so that it has a similar meaning to the first sentence, using the word given. Do not change the word given. You must use between three and six words, including the word given.

2 I've realised that I can't trust him as much as I had thought.
LESS
I've realised he .... I had thought.

3 I'm still not sure which TV I want to buy.
MIND
I haven't .... yet about which TV I want to buy.

4 It's possible that a storm was responsible for the blackout.
BY
The blackout could .... a storm.

5 When I spend my money on gadgets, my happiness increases.
THE
The .... I feel.

6 It's annoying that so many manufacturers no longer include paper instructions.
AWAY
It's annoying that so many manufacturers .... paper instructions.

VOCABULARY AND READING
FILMS AND BOOKS

1 Correct the mistakes in the words or phrases or put a tick by any you think are correct.

1 blerb	7 masterpiese
2 blockbuster	8 remake
3 box-office flopp	9 revanue
4 cinemagor	10 sequel
5 installment	11 set in
6 main caracter	12 trailler

2 Match the definitions to the answers from Exercise 1.

1 a film that is unsuccessful
2 a new version of an old film
3 a person who regularly watches films at the cinema
4 a book or film that is very successful
5 the most important person in a book or film

6 a book or film that is made with a huge amount of skill
7 one of several parts which a story or series is divided into
8 describing where and when the story happens
9 the money that a film company makes from a movie
10 an advertisement for a film consisting of short parts from it
11 a short description of a book or film that is intended to make people want to read or see it
12 a book or film that continues the story of a previous one

3 Complete the email with the words and phrases from Exercise 1.

4 Look at these film posters. What do they have in common?

5 Why do screenplay writers choose to adapt a work of fiction for TV? What process do they go through? Make a list of your ideas and then read the article on the opposite page quickly to check.

6 Read the article about adaptations again. Six paragraphs have been removed from the article. Choose from the paragraphs A–G the one which fits each gap (1–6). There is one extra paragraph which you do not need to use.

7 Match the highlighted words in the text to the meanings.

1 unfamiliar with someone/something
2 something that you cannot stop once you have started

3 having lost confidence/hope
4 ambitious/hopeful
5 dealing with a constant supply of something

Hey Gael,

I had the most amazing dream last night. Well, not that amazing, considering that I'm such a keen
1 .... and must see at least fifteen films each month … but, anyway, it was pretty special.

So, in the dream I was a famous actor and I was playing the 2 .... in Martin Scorsese's new film. Well, kind of new, it was actually a 3 .... of his classic, *Taxi Driver,* which he originally made all the way back in 1976. You know that film, right? The one 4 .... New York. It's an absolute
5 .... – I love it so much. In the dream, Scorsese was telling me that if our film generated enough 6 ...., he'd get me back next year to act in the 7 .... to *The Irishman*, which was a huge success last year. He said that he'd never intended to write a second 8 .... to the story, but he had such a good feeling about me that he couldn't wait to get started!

Anyway, next thing I know, I'm sitting in the cinema, watching a couple of 9 .... for some other movies, when a voice on screen says, 'Now, from director Martin Scorsese, the new *Taxi Driver*, starring Emile Duncan.' Everyone in the cinema turned to me and cheered!

Unfortunately, in the next part of the dream I was back at college. Rather than being a huge
10 .... that millions of people had paid to see, the film had been a total 11 ....
and Martin didn't want me to act in any more of his films, ever again.

Never mind! I'm going back to reading the 12 .... of the next movie I'm planning to watch.

Speak soon,

Emile

The Art of Adaptation

Producing TV adaptations of novels requires a particular set of skills, but it can be very rewarding, writes Jade Hamlet.

It's been a long day. You turn on the TV and are bombarded with options for what to watch. When a particular show or series happens to catch your attention, you'd be forgiven for thinking to yourself, 'I've seen that before … haven't I?' But when you check, you discover that it is a brand new production. Well, you sigh, that's all you get on TV these days: remakes and new adaptations of novels that we have seen many times previously.

> **1**

One issue is that attracting viewers to watch something new is a huge challenge. They'll be entirely unacquainted with the storyline, the characters will be strangers to them, and even if they watch a trailer, they will still have little idea of either. With something that's unfamiliar, you must convince the audience to spend time with imagined individuals who they have absolutely no existing connection to.

> **2**

So, the difficulty with original scripts lies more in promoting them than in writing them. In fact, it is far easier to make a movie based on a novel than it is to create something new. For any aspiring screenplay writer coming expectantly into the TV and movie industry, this is often a depressing realisation. And yet, actually, it is a luxury to be able to borrow the title of a celebrated book for an adaptation.

> **3**

Adaptations, in this way – and somewhat ironically – give you the chance to create something entirely personal. When I adapted Don Quixote for television, I read the first part from cover to cover three times, then put it completely to one side. With a few notes I'd made about the plot, and a strong memory of the best scenes in the book, I began to write. I did exactly the same for the second part of the book, and eventually, we had a TV script. That's how you adapt a novel for the screen.

> **4**

So, when last year I came to adapt my own novel into a television series, did I follow the same steps? I tried to but struggled. I'd worked on that novel for years and built its world from nothing. A city-centre park, which I had so vividly imagined and described so carefully in the novel, became little more than a simple noun in the screenplay – 'park'. Characters became mere names on a page, the narratives became trivial and I became disheartened.

> **5**

I also had to accept that, at some point later, the director might insist on removing a scene or cutting out one of the people in the story. And I would need to put my emotions to one side. To keep something in, I'd need to argue the case without sentiment and with an objective approach. Of course, there is also the possibility that the director might actually be right.

> **6**

Ultimately, I will keep writing screenplays for whoever wants to make or see them. It is a slow-yet-rapid, easy-yet-impossible, original-yet-adapted process that makes my job so addictive.

A The thing is, they often are. Sometimes as a writer, you have to swallow your pride and accept that the people you are working with are experienced professionals who know how to communicate something on screen better than you do.

B While there are many people who might find this concept difficult to understand, it is entirely obvious if you stop to consider what an adaptation is actually supposed to do. Or rather, what it is not supposed to do.

C One possible explanation is that writers today are simply incapable of creating original screenplays. The reality is, however, that many writers much prefer to craft their own scripts than to adapt one. Also, TV production companies are often desperate to make original drama. So, what's the problem?

D And it is that which grabs the audience's attention – a person, or a phrase, that is familiar to them. If we have the viewer's attention, we have an audience. And, if we have an audience, we can show the world how skilled and original we are as writers.

E Of course, the process is slightly more complicated than that, but the point remains the same. Stay faithful to your own interpretation of a book, be prepared to remove almost all detail, and you'll get to the essential point of the story and the characters.

F Now consider the adaptation. If I say the word 'Frankenstein', there are no such problems. Those same viewers will have an image, a narrative, perhaps a memory of the book. They don't need an advertisement, or a poster, to decide whether or not they fancy watching it.

G Eventually, however, you have to realise this: if you treasure every word or aren't prepared to sacrifice parts of your characters, that's when the trouble starts. You must approach your creation with a cold heart, almost as if you are reading it for the first time. Only then will you have your adaptation.

GRAMMAR
GERUNDS AND INFINITIVES

1 Complete the table with the verbs in the box.

afford   can't stand   claim   consider   continue   finish   forget   happen
imagine   intend   keep   mean   prefer   remember   stop   try

Followed by gerund	Followed by *to* + infinitive	Followed by gerund or *to* + infinitive

2 Choose the correct options.

1 I'd love to come to the cinema on Saturday, but I can't even afford *to buy / buying* a ticket, unfortunately.
2 If I finally finish *to write / writing* my novel, I'll send it to some publishers.
3 Will Smith attempted *to bring / bringing* humour to the movie, but the rest of the cast weren't funny at all.
4 Whenever I start a new series, I can't help *to watch / watching* at least four episodes in a row.
5 Michele has finally decided *applying / to apply* to film school – I think he'd make a great director.
6 I don't think Henry even wants to learn Portuguese. He keeps *saying / to say* he's going to quit his classes.
7 To learn new vocabulary from an English-language film, it helps *to keep / keeping* a notebook by your side.
8 I do enjoy living in the countryside these days, but I really miss *going / to go* to the theatre.

3 Complete the sentences with the gerund or *to* + infinitive form of the verb. If both forms are possible, with no change in meaning, put a tick in the gap.

0 GO
  A Sorry, we haven't got any milk for the coffee. I forgot *to go* to the shops earlier.
  B Even in his old age, Paco never forgot *going* to the theatre for the first time.
1 PLAY
  A I prefer _____ team sports – you meet lots of interesting people.
  B Most of my friends prefer _____ video games with other people, rather than on their own.
2 LOOK
  A I don't really care about my appearance. I stopped _____ in the mirror ages ago.
  B When we were in Athens, we must have stopped _____ at every single monument.
3 GET
  A Having a conversation in English will continue _____ easier the more you practise.
  B We won't be able to go out if the weather continues _____ worse.
4 PUT
  A When I get home later, I must remember _____ my gym kit in the wash.
  B I have no idea where your keys are. Do you remember _____ them in your bag?

4 Complete the sentences with the gerund or *to* + infinitive form of the verbs in the box. You may need to add a preposition.

complain   hear   know   listen
meet   ~~see~~   visit   watch   write

0 After he had finished the fifth level, Michael was surprised *to see* his name at the top of the leader board.
1 I think I saw Antonio Banderas at the airport, but it was difficult _____ for sure.
2 My mum is getting so excited about _____ Málaga.
3 When he got to college, he was shocked _____ that his favourite teacher had just quit.
4 _____ to a podcast at night is the only thing that helps me to fall asleep.
5 George R. R. Martin is most famous for _____ novels, but he also spent time as a script writer for TV.
6 The food was great, but you were right _____ to the manager – the service was awful.
7 Since she's such an introvert, Raquel finds it difficult to get enthusiastic _____ new people.
8 I really feel like _____ a silly action movie tonight.

5 Correct the mistakes in the sentences or put a tick by any you think are correct.

1 Successful people work very hard to reach their goals.

2 There is certainly a need of preparing yourself for each time you walk out on stage.
3 You need to leave earlier for arriving at the theatre on time.
4 There's a lot of pressure on tonight's performance. We won't get another chance do it again.
5 We strongly recommend building a path between the rehearsal room and the studio.
6 I love being at the theatre, as well as go to the cinema.

7 I won't be able to help you preparing for your audition.

8 The writers are overworked and refuse to take on more responsibilities.

6 Complete these sentences so that they are true for you.

1 When I leave school, I want to keep _____ .
2 I really enjoy _____ .
3 I often forget _____ .
4 One day, I'd love to try _____ .

VOCABULARY
ENTERTAINMENT: ADVERB AND ADJECTIVE COLLOCATIONS

1 Match the adverbs to the adjectives to make collocations.

1 largely
2 highly
3 hysterically
4 critically
5 painfully
6 internationally

a acclaimed
b unknown
c slow
d anticipated
e successful
f funny

1 .... 2 .... 3 .... 4 .... 5 .... 6 ....

2 Complete the sentences with a collocation from Exercise 1.

1 If you read his reviews, it becomes clear that Steven Spielberg is one of the most .... directors. He's highly respected by everyone in the industry.
2 I found *The Caps* .... I almost nodded off in the cinema.
3 Cinemagoers are preparing themselves and looking forward to the .... sequel to the blockbuster hit, *The Locks.*
4 Lots of actors dream of becoming .... – known and loved by millions of film fans all over the world.
5 *Up and Over* is .... – I was in tears of laughter.
6 Lady Gaga was once was a .... actor working as a part-time waiter. Now, she's world-famous.

ENTERTAINMENT: COMPOUND ADJECTIVES

3 Write the compound adjectives used to talk about films. Use the definitions and the initial letters in brackets to help you.

0 known across the globe (WF) *world-famous*
1 full of explosions and fast cars (AP) ....
2 given prizes by judges, fans or critics (AW) ....
3 made for a smaller amount of money than most films (LB) ....
4 on the judges' list as a possible winner of an Academy Award (ON) ....
5 makes the audience reflect carefully on life (TP) ....
6 seen more or more profitable than any other film (RB) ....
7 the most recognised or popular film (BK) ....
8 receiving the most amount of money to do a job (HP) ....

4 Complete the sentences from film and book reviews with answers from Exercises 1–3.

1 It was a really .... novel. It made me think a lot about life and what I want to achieve.
2 *Avengers: Endgame* was a .... success at the box office, bringing in over a billion dollars on its first weekend.
3 Despite the cast being .... , their performances were excellent. I can't believe I'd never heard of them before.
4 I tend to prefer quiet, ... films which don't spend a lot of money on car chases and special effects.
5 As much as it pains me to say, this .... new collection of short stories from Dario Gilby fails to live up to expectations.
6 There's no guarantee of writing a .... book, as you never know what is going to please professional reviewers.
7 Although his .... work is probably *One Hundred Years of Solitude*, Gabriel García Márquez produced other writing of far superior quality, in my opinion.
8 To make a great movie, you don't necessarily need a .... superstar who is recognised all over the globe.
9 Despite being an .... actor who was even .... a few years ago (although he didn't win, in the end), Peter Malan has since found good roles difficult to get.
10 While the main characters were well acted, I found the storyline .... ; the movie should have been at least half an hour shorter.
11 One of the .... actors working today is Dwayne Johnson – he earned $89.4 million in 2019.
12 From the opening scene to the end credits, I was crying with laughter at this .... comedy from Steve Carell.

5 Answer the questions.

1 What was the last critically acclaimed movie you watched?
....
2 If you met a world-famous actor, what would you say to them?
....
3 Do you think Oscar-nominated films are better? Why? / Why not?
....
4 What is the most thought-provoking film you have seen?
....
5 Do you prefer action-packed or low-budget movies? Why?
....

WRITING
A REVIEW

» SEE *PREPARE TO WRITE* BOX, STUDENT'S BOOK PAGE 49

1 Read the paragraph from a book review. What do you notice about the language used in bold?

> I particularly enjoyed the **interesting tales** of life at that time and the story from start to finish was **really interesting**. I felt like I was being taken back to a time and a place that was **totally unlike** our world today. It really **talks about the past in an interesting and believable way**. If you **like reading** historical novels, you will **really love** this book with its **good conversations** and **good observations and descriptions** of life in nineteenth-century America.

2 Match the higher-level phrases to the phrases in bold from Exercise 1.

1 extremely gripping
2 enjoy losing yourself in
3 vivid narratives
4 completely fall for
5 lively dialogues
6 realistic accounts
7 radically different from
8 brings the past to life

3 Correct any mistakes in the phrases below or put a tick by the ones you think are correct. Then add them to the table.

1 In brief,
2 Overall,
3 In a summary,
4 All things regarded,
5 My impression is
6 In short,
7 The only downpart was
8 In the whole,
9 To summarise up,
10 Taking all into consideration,
11 Personally, I feel that
12 To my thoughts,
13 What I (dis)like is
14 To be fair,
15 In my private view,
16 What impressed me most

Summarising	Giving opinions

4 Are these opinions positive or negative? Write *P* (positive) or *N* (negative) next to each one.

1 'It's not like the majority of other films I've seen.'
2 'It was so obvious what was going to happen in the end.'
3 'I felt like I'd really understood someone else's mind.'
4 'I didn't stop laughing once.'
5 'I was so bored from start to finish.'
6 'The special effects were astonishing.'
7 'I've seen films like this a million times before.'
8 'Everything I saw seemed so unlikely to happen in real life.'
9 'I couldn't take my eyes off the screen.'
10 'I was hoping for something quite serious, but, in fact, it wasn't at all.'

5 Match the adjectives to the opinions 1–10 in Exercise 4. Use a dictionary if you need to.

A predictable   *2*
B dazzling
C clichéd
D insightful
E far-fetched

F absorbing
G superficial
H hilarious
I original
J tedious

6 Read the task. How many questions do you need to address?

> Send us a review of a book or movie that is set in the past. How well did the book or movie tell the story? How effectively did it describe that time in history? Was there anything that you particularly enjoyed/disliked?
> Write your **review.**

7 Read the answer to the task in Exercise 8, ignoring the gaps. Has the student answered all the questions?

8 Complete the review with words and phrases from this section.

> In the internationally-successful novel, *The House of One Hundred Clocks*, the reader follows the ¹ a_____ story of a girl called Helena, who moves with her father into a house where there are – no great surprise – one hundred clocks, which they must never allow to stop. Why? Well, that is what Helena is determined to find out. This mystery drives the ² v_____ narrative forward and ³ b_____ the p_____ to l_____ in wonderful and surprising ways.
>
> In my ⁴ p_____ v_____, we are provided with an insightful look at another moment in history and a character I could completely identify with, even though her world at that time is ⁵ r_____ d_____ from ours today. The book is set at the start of the 20th century and we get to experience what life was like back then, not only by imagining being surrounded by ticking clocks and huge, colourful dresses, but also by understanding how women at that time had so few rights. It explores the theme of time in a number of ⁶ t_____ – p_____ ways, and you believe what you are reading, even though the plot is a little ⁷ f_____ – f_____.
>
> What impressed me most was the way that the writer was able to create an ⁸ e_____ g_____ story that, in many ways, provides a ⁹ r_____ a_____ of life 120 years ago. This is even more enjoyable when accompanied with the fantasy elements of the book.
>
> The House of One Hundred Clocks has received high praise from reviewers, and it is easy to see why. To my ¹⁰ _____, it works perfectly on a number of levels. I'm in no doubt that I'll pick it up again at some point in the future.

The
House
of
One Hundred Clocks

A.M.Howell

🔍 5   ♡ 20   ⬚ 9   Purchase book

★★★★☆
4 out of 5 stars

9 Write an answer to the question below. Write your review in 220–260 words.

> Send us a review of a movie that is set in the future. How well did the movie tell the story? How believable was the representation of the future? Was there anything that you particularly enjoyed/disliked?
> Write your **review.**

7 AGAINST ALL ODDS

VOCABULARY AND READING
CHALLENGES AND ACHIEVEMENTS

1 **Choose the correct option in each sentence.**

1 A Running a marathon is a test of *against all odds / endurance* that should not be attempted without a strict training regime.
   B She injured herself in the warm-up but, *against all odds / endurance*, managed to win in the end.

2 A After a slow start, the experienced Brazil team *overcame / thrived* their determined opponents.
   B Mido gained in confidence and *overcame / thrived* as he played more often in the first team.

3 A Many sportspeople are at their best when dealing with a certain amount of *setbacks / adversity*, such as losing heavily – it is often what motivates them.
   B She suffered a great number of *setbacks / adversity* early in her career – mostly injuries.

4 A Having huge amounts of *self-belief / self-discipline* is vital if you want to become an elite athlete. Listen only to yourself, not your critics.
   B Many hopeful sportspeople lack the *self-belief / self-discipline* to turn their hobby into a career, often because they can't deal with the intense training.

5 A Throughout her career, Serena Williams has *broken down barriers / suffered a defeat* and achieved great things both on and off the court.
   B Bayern Munich only have three games left to play this season, and they still haven't *broken down barriers / suffered a defeat*.

2 **Match the definitions to the words or phrases from Exercise 1.**

1 achieve something despite being unlikely to succeed ....
2 something that happens which prevents a process from happening ....
3 the ability to keep doing something difficult, unpleasant or painful for a long time ....
4 improve understanding and communication between people who have different opinions ....
5 the ability to make yourself do things you know you should do, even when you do not want to ....
6 grow, develop or be successful ....
7 succeed in dealing with a problem or difficulty; defeat an opponent ....
8 a difficult or unlucky situation or event ....
9 trust in your own abilities ....
10 get beaten by an opponent ....

3 **Complete the sentences with the words or phrases from Exercises 1 and 2.**

1 Following a national team can often help to .... between fans of opposing football clubs.
2 Cambridge United suffered a serious .... in their attempt to become champions when they were beaten 4–1 last night.
3 My brother likes to run in long-distance .... races.
4 Their best players were all sold at the start of the season. However, ..., they were champions by the end of it.
5 The best sportspeople seem to .... when under pressure.
6 He struggled to .... his fitness problems and was never the same player again, sadly.
7 I wanted to play golf professionally when I was younger, but didn't have enough .... – I liked going out too much.
8 Despite the .... she faced when growing up in a poor neighbourhood, she still made it to the top.
9 Rafa Nadal .... his first defeat of the year yesterday.
10 Without huge amounts of .... telling you that you can be number one, you will never become a top athlete.

4 **Read the quotation below. What do you think it means?**

'The more I practise, the luckier I get.'

5 **Read the article on the opposite page quickly. What is the best title?**

A Useful research practices in sports science
B The importance of self-belief in sport
C Contributing factors in sporting success

6 **Read the article again. Which two theories are *not* discussed in the text?**

1 The more you focus on one sport when you are young, the more likely you are to succeed.
2 The more competition there is in sport, the more likely young people are to succeed.
3 The more sports you try when you are young, the more likely you are to succeed.
4 The more encouragement young people receive in sport, the more likely they are to succeed.
5 The more open young people are to self-improvement, the more likely they are to succeed.

For a number of decades now, sports scientists have debated how and why some young sportspeople clearly have more motivation than others. This often used to be discussed with references to 'talent', 'hunger' and 'ambition', but these words will only take us so far in our quest to understand the phenomenon completely.

There was always a belief that those at the top of the sporting tree, for the most part, have their DNA to thank for their achievements. But at the start of the 21st century, a new theory began to command the attention of the public: the only difference between those athletes who have reached the top and those who never will is that anyone operating at the highest level has simply practised more. To become a success, the hypothesis went, a sportsperson must aim to spend at least 10,000 hours of *deliberate practice* on one discipline. This suggests that the earlier you start and the more often you practise, the better your chances of success will be. However, if we look more closely at the science, we will see this claim is not supported. 1

2   But what, exactly? To understand, it helps to consider a 2011 Danish study which compared 148 elite athletes who were then at the height of their powers to 95 *near-elite* athletes who had not quite attained the same levels of success. The academics focused on a vast range of disciplines, from canoeing to skiing to triathlon and more. They showed that, when compared with the elite group, the near-elite athletes had actually spent a far greater number of hours on the training field between the ages of nine and fifteen. They had also begun competing at national and international levels earlier. And yet, none of this actually mattered in the long run. 3

4

Perhaps because the deliberate practice model focuses so attentively on one sport, the young sportsperson, at some point, simply begins to lose interest. It could also be that, with their physical development put under intense early strain, they become injured and over-tired. At the same time, those who become elite later tend to enjoy a different start to their sporting careers. They are less likely to participate in intensive, structured coaching sessions. Also, rather than focusing on building up a bank of hours in one sport, they vary the number of pursuits they take part in and thus develop a wide range of skills which they transfer to other areas. 5

6

We also need to consider the idea of mental attitude. In 1978, Carol Dweck, professor of psychology at Stanford University, carried out an important experiment that is still talked about today. After giving 150 students a questionnaire, the results showed they could be divided into two groups. The first group believed that talent or intelligence is essentially genetic (*fixed mindset*), and the second considered that these qualities can always be improved (*growth mindset*). When all of the students were provided with 12 tricky problems to solve, the fixed mindset group quickly began to blame themselves for their struggles, while the growth mindset team did not focus in any way on their own shortcomings. 7

8

If we make the link, we understand that a promising sportsperson with a fixed mindset may view any future success as being largely to do with innate talent. So, during any early success, they may become convinced that they have the right genes and relax the intensity or frequency of their training. At the same time, if they find that they are losing more often than winning, they are more likely to believe that their opponents are more naturally gifted than they are and give up. If their opponents possess more innate talent, they will never be able to overcome them. On the other hand, if they truly believe in their abilities to improve and therefore to thrive – the growth mindset – they will increase their efforts. They view any failure as providing the chance to adapt and grow, and they will eventually succeed. 9

7 **Read the article again and match the sentences A–I to the correct positions (1–9) in the text.**

A This change in position can occur for a number of reasons. _____

B The connection to sport is clear. _____

C In other words, they sample what is out there on offer before eventually settling on one sport. _____

D The elites overtook them in late adolescence and never looked back. _____

E There are clearly other factors involved. _____

F Again, though, we cannot expect one theory to explain everything. _____

G This kind of attitude is pivotal to any successful sporting development. _____

H In fact, the idea that they were failing never occurred to them. _____

I Deliberate practice alone is not enough. _____

8 **Match the highlighted words in the article to the meanings.**

1 reach or succeed in getting something _____

2 an established set of attitudes that someone holds _____

3 a particular area of interest or study _____

4 activities you spend time doing _____

5 a fault or failure to reach a particular standard _____

GRAMMAR
CONDITIONALS

1 Match the sentence halves.

1 If he doesn't get fit after his long-term injury,
2 If he plays well,
3 If she hadn't got injured when she was 16,
4 Unless he changes his tactics,
5 If he wasn't admired by his teammates,
6 If her concentration hadn't been perfect,
7 If he weren't so obsessed with football,

a he'll lose this match in the next ten minutes.
b he wouldn't be captain of the team.
c she'd be playing for Atlético by now.
d he wouldn't have spent all that money on a ticket.
e she might have found it more difficult to win.
f his team usually wins.
g he might not ever play again.

| 1 ...... | 3 ...... | 5 ...... | 7 ...... |
| 2 ...... | 4 ...... | 6 ...... | |

2 Match the sentences in Exercise 1 to the rules.

A zero conditional ......
B 1st conditional ...... and ......
C 2nd conditional ......
D 3rd conditional ......
E mixed conditional ...... and ......

3 Choose the correct options.

1 That was an amazing goal. If we *haven't / hadn't* seen it with our own eyes, I wouldn't have believed it could happen.
2 If I *could / can* afford the course fees, I'd love to play at the RC Valderrama golf course.
3 She often does an extra hour of training if *she'll have / she has* enough energy at the end of the session.
4 If the rain hadn't been so heavy last night, there *will / would* still be a match to play this afternoon.
5 *I'd / I'll* let you know if I end up going to the match tomorrow.
6 They might win more matches if they *wouldn't / didn't* always let in late goals.

4 Complete the sentences with the verbs in brackets in the correct form. There may be more than one correct answer.

1 If they .... (not spend) so much money on players last summer, they wouldn't be champions now.
2 If I hadn't played so much at school, I .... (never become) so good at netball.
3 If he .... (listen) more to his coach when he was young, he'd be as famous as Ronaldo.
4 If negative thoughts ever .... (come) into my head, I just try to ignore them.
5 They would have won if half of their team .... (not be) injured.
6 I think I .... (go) for a run later if it's not too hot.
7 She .... (find) it easier to win if she spent more time practising her technique.

5 Complete the sentences with the correct word pair (A–F) in the correct form. In each word pair, it is indicated whether you need to use a positive (+) or a negative (-) form.

0 If I _had looked after_ myself more when I was young, I _would have been_ fitter as an adult.
1 Anyone can .... sport to a high standard if they .... hard enough.
2 I don't think I .... allowed to come to the match with you unless my parents .... it's okay.
3 If I .... my subscription to the sports channel, I .... that amazing race yesterday.
4 I .... for another team, even if they .... me all the money in the world.
5 If you .... as hard as you can, the coaching staff .... you every step of the way.
6 What would we .... every weekend if TV .... ?

A + be / + say	E - cancel / + see
B + train / + support	F + play / + work
C - play / + offer	G + look after / + be
D + do / + invent	

6 Correct the mistakes in the sentences or put a tick by any you think are correct.

1 She chose to play basketball over football in the end. What would you do if you had been in her position? ....
2 We would appreciate if you could give us further details about how to get to the stadium. ....
3 If you became a famous athlete, you would have to sign a lot of autographs. ....
4 I often think about what would my life be like if I hadn't followed my ambitions. ....
5 If there will be three or more goals, people will be entertained and everyone will go home happy. ....
6 Yesterday, I was thinking about how boring life would be if I hadn't joined the basketball team. ....

7 Rewrite the sentences using the second, third or mixed conditional.

0 I'm not at home because I didn't realise how late it was.
If I had realised how late it was, I'd be at home now.
1 People are inspired to get fit because sports stars act as good role models.
If sports stars didn't act as good role models, ...
2 Training was so hard this morning – I feel exhausted now.
I .... if training hadn't been so hard this morning.
3 I don't go to the gym often because I don't find it enjoyable.
If I found going to the gym enjoyable, ...
4 I only play tennis with Felix because I usually beat him.
I .... if I didn't usually beat him.
5 She is recognised as one of the world's best because she was so determined in her early years.
If she hadn't been so determined in her early years, ...
6 They won the final comfortably because they didn't panic after letting in the first goal.
They wouldn't ....

VOCABULARY
NOUN SUFFIXES

1 Choose the correct suffix to make these words into nouns or adjectives.

accept   accurate   adaptable   ~~aggressive~~   child   censor
conscious   exaggerate   free   jealous   occur   replace   survive

-al	-ance	-cy	-dom	-ence
-hood	**-ity**	**-ment**	**-ness**	**-ship**
-(s)ion	**-(t)ion**	**-y**		
aggression				

2 Complete the words with the correct suffix from the table in Exercise 1.

1 I truly believe that any harass_____ of the referee should result in a penalty to the opposition.
2 In the UK, there is always an explo_____ of interest in tennis during the Wimbledon tournament.
3 He is obsessed with watching sport, so didn't question for a moment the renew_____ of his *GameTV* subscription.
4 There are too many disturb_____ to the flow of football matches these days, thanks to video technology constantly reviewing every decision.
5 The hospital_____ industry plays an important part in ensuring that spectators enjoy sporting events.
6 Seeing huge transfer fees for footballers is an extremely common occur_____ these days.

3 Complete the sentences with the correct form of the words in the box.

admit   agile   encourage   guide   likely   refuse

1 Sportspeople generally perform better if they have received clear tactical _____ from their coaches.
2 She always played better if she could hear words of _____ from her friends in the crowd.
3 His boxing skills are legendary, but many say it was Muhammad Ali's _____ to accept defeat that made him a champion.
4 He held his hands up to the sky in a clear _____ that he had acted against the rules of the sport.
5 I can never quite believe it when I watch gymnasts live – their _____ is unbelievable.
6 The _____ of any team winning the Davis Cup three times in a row is pretty small.

4 Complete the sentences with the words in the box in the correct form.

efficient   lonely   refer   wise

1 It is common for athletes to question the _____ of their decision to retire at an early age.
2 Many elite athletes suffer from _____ after they reach a certain level of fame.
3 She beat her opponent in a great display of _____, taking only 40 minutes to win the match.
4 In sport, your talent is on display. You don't need a _____ from a previous employer to get a job.

5 For questions 1–8, read the text below. Use the word given in capitals at the end of some of the lines to form a word that fits in the gap in the same line.

MEDIEVAL **FOOTBALL**

In modern games of football, when there is unfair play or **(0)** *interference* , a foul is usually given. At this point, the opposition have to move away from the ball in **(1)** _____ for the free kick to be taken. And, while there may be a few bruises here and there, the games tend to reach their **(2)** _____ with the players all in one piece. — INTERFERE / READY / CONCLUDE

It was very different in medieval times. The **(3)** _____ of being awarded a free kick was minimal, and the astonishing levels of violence meant each game was often more about personal **(4)** _____ than victory. Any spectators may have experienced periods of extreme **(5)** _____ during the match, partly because the two goals could be up to five kilometres away from each other, while the weight of the ball meant that it could not be kicked with any great **(6)** _____ or power. Interestingly, we know from a number of accounts and **(7)** _____ to the game written at that time that crowds would often encourage **(8)** _____ on the pitch – just to have something to watch. — LIKELY / SURVIVE / BORE / ACCURATE / REFER / DISTURB

LISTENING

1 Have you taken up a new sport recently? What do you think are people's main reasons for taking up a new sport? Make a list.

....

....

....

2 Which of the following quotations (1–3) is the closest in meaning to option A? Which words helped you choose?

A to overcome feelings of anxiety

1 'I'd just lost my job and was starting to feel pretty bored.'
2 '"Go on, then, weigh yourself," she said. I was shocked at how much it actually was.'
3 ' … my focus was on controlling my nerves whenever I was close to the edge of a lake or a river.'

 3 Read the questions in Task One and Task Two. You will hear five short extracts in which people are talking about taking up a new sport. For speakers 1–5, choose from the list (A–H). As you listen, you should complete both tasks.

TASK ONE

For questions 1–5, choose from the list (A–H) each speaker's main reason for taking up the new sport.

A to overcome feelings of anxiety
B to impress a family member
C to challenge their existing beliefs
D to fulfil a childhood ambition
E to settle a continuing argument
F to improve physical fitness
G to give themselves a distraction
H to set a good example to others

1 Speaker 1 ....
2 Speaker 2 ....
3 Speaker 3 ....
4 Speaker 4 ....
5 Speaker 5 ....

TASK TWO

For questions 6–10, choose from the list (A–H) what each speaker has found satisfying about taking up the new sport.

A It has justified a financial investment.
B It has led to a review of their spending patterns.
C It has enhanced the quality of a relationship.
D It has created a connection with nature.
E It has expanded their social network.
F It has led to improved job opportunities.
G It has increased their respect for elite athletes.
H It has encouraged them to create an exercise plan.

6 Speaker 1 ....
7 Speaker 2 ....
8 Speaker 3 ....
9 Speaker 4 ....
10 Speaker 5 ....

 4 Listen again and complete these phrases from the extracts.

1 'A friend at the place where I'd been working invited me for a game of squash, and I thought, "great, it'll .... feeling like this for a while," and it really did.

2 'Earlier this year, we decided to find out .... who's the best.'

3 'I had no right to be instructing them to .... unless I could demonstrate to them how important it really is.'

4 'I got such an unexpected sense of feeling .... in the environment around me, I almost forgot that I was supposed to be pushing off and heading downhill.'

5 'It's so much more than something to do at the weekend. It's great that it .... my health and fitness'.

5 Match the definitions to the answers from Exercise 4.

1 keep yourself in good physical condition
....

2 allow you to stop worrying about a particular thing
....

3 cause big improvements or have a very good effect
....

4 completely and in a way that will finally solve a problem
....

5 happy because you feel that you belong in the place or situation you are in
....

6 Answer the questions so they are true for you.

1 The best way for me to stay in shape is to ....

2 If I need to take my mind off my studies, I usually ....

3 I can guarantee that I'll feel completely at one with my surroundings when I'm in ....

4 It's generally true that .... works wonders for my state of mind.

5 One day, I would really love to .... once and for all.

1 Rewrite the following sentence twice by rephrasing the words in *italics*.

Before I do anything, I *prefer to assess* the situation.

I _____ of a situation before I do anything.

I _____ of a situation before I do anything.

2 Complete the sentence with a six-word phrase including the word *cons*.

Before I do anything, I *prefer to assess* the situation.

I _____ of a situation before I do anything.

3 Look at the question below. Is it possible to use the exact same words as the answer to Exercise 2? Why? / Why not?

1 I've recently spent a lot of time assessing whether I want to go vegan.

CONS

I've recently been _____ of going vegan.

4 For questions 2–6, complete the second sentence so that it has a similar meaning to the first sentence, using the word given. Do not change the word given. You must use between three and six words, including the word given.

2 Although he was in his eighties, he continued to play football regularly.

ON

He _____ being in his eighties.

3 I wouldn't have achieved what I did without all the encouragement of my parents.

SO

If my parents _____ encouragement, I wouldn't have achieved what I did.

4 The government's new policy has created incredible feelings of hostility in the public.

TOWARDS

A huge number of people _____ the government's new policy.

5 It was obvious that he was going to get sweaty, running in 40-degree heat.

BROKE

Running in 40-degree heat, it's no wonder _____ sweat.

6 Next week is the ten-year anniversary of No Direction performing in the same band.

TOGETHER

By next week, No Direction _____ for ten years.

5 Read the text in Exercise 8 quickly. What do you think the title means?

6 How many prepositions/adverbs do you need to use to complete the text?

7 Use the prepositions in the box to complete five of the gaps in Exercise 8.

> against   ahead   at   down
> for   in   to   towards   with

8 Complete the remaining gaps. Use only one word in each gap.

BOUNCING BACK

Suffering a long-term injury is easily **(0)** _one_ of the most frustrating things that can happen to an athlete. When I damaged my left knee ligaments, I immediately knew that it was a huge cause **(1)** _____ concern. In fact, some of my team-mates were convinced that the injury **(2)** _____ mean the end of my career as a professional athlete. My coach, however, assured me that I still had a future in the sport. If **(3)** _____ hadn't been for her, I might well have given up.

The problem was, I completely lacked self-belief. If I felt myself losing the battle against my injury, my coach used to say to me, 'you're doing so well – a long road still lies **(4)** _____ of you, but you must keep going.' So often, I felt like I had **(5)** _____ a brick wall and started believing that all my efforts had gone **(6)** _____ the drain. But then I realised that everyone is faced **(7)** _____ adversity at some point in life. It's how you deal with it that makes you a winner. Doubt had made me feel inferior **(8)** _____ my opponents before. I wasn't going to let it win again …

8 MAKING ENDS MEET

1 Complete the words with the missing vowels.

1 _u_ n _a_ ff _o_ rd _a_ bl _e_
2 t_ _k_ _ _ _t_ _ _l_ _ _n
3 r_ _p_ – _ _ff
4 _ _ll_ _w_ _nc
5 s_ _pp_ _rt
6 w_ _ll_ – _ _ff
7 w_ _thdr_ _w
8 br_ _k
9 f_ _nd

2 Match the definitions to the words or phrases from Exercise 1.

1 too expensive to buy ....
2 having a lot of money or resources ....
3 take out money from a machine or bank ....
4 an amount of money given regularly for a particular purpose ....
5 financial help ....
6 provide the money to pay for something ....
7 borrow money from a bank ....
8 something that is not worth the money you pay for it ....
9 without money ....

3 Complete the sentences with the words from Exercise 1 in the correct form.

1 Owning or renting a city centre apartment is completely .... for someone on an average income.
2 The company has agreed to .... my research trip to China.
3 I couldn't have managed at college if I hadn't received an .... from my parents.
4 My family has never been ...., but we'd never consider ourselves as poor, either.
5 Fewer and fewer people .... money these days, thanks to cashless, contactless card payment.
6 If you are having financial difficulties, you can apply for .... from the government.
7 We'll need to .... from the bank if business doesn't improve soon.
8 My broadband package is a total ...., but I can't get out of my contract until next year.
9 It'd be great to come out with you this evening, but I've not had any work recently and I'm completely ....

4 Read the four texts on the opposite page quickly. Write each person's name next to the roles 1–4.

1 child/adolescent psychotherapist ....
2 new graduate about to get a job ....
3 young entrepreneur ....
4 recruitment agent ....

5 Read the reports on the opposite page again. For questions 1–10, choose from the four people (A–D). The people may be chosen more than once.

Which person

1 admits that young people may have unreasonable expectations? ....
2 praises a unique characteristic of a particular group of people? ....
3 expresses moral disapproval of certain working practices? ....
4 identifies a key factor for achieving success at work? ....
5 recommends a technological solution to an outdated process? ....
6 argues that a particular impression of young people is false? ....
7 describes being confused by an apparent contradiction? ....
8 urges employers to be honest when dealing with prospective new staff? ....
9 mentions how good intentions can have unexpectedly negative consequences? ....
10 expresses a wish not to follow a strict working schedule? ....

6 Match the highlighted words to the meanings.

1 understand ....
2 changing an opinion/view ....
3 a series of activities to try to achieve something ....
4 stop giving your attention to something ....
5 used after a negative phrase to add emphasis to the idea that is being expressed ....

Ⓐ ERICA

Having just finished my university studies, I'm not expecting to earn much initially, but money is definitely a motivating factor for me, and I'd be perfectly happy to work evenings or weekends for higher pay. It would also be great to have flexibility because the idea of being in the office from nine to five has no appeal for me whatsoever. I think that's becoming the case everywhere now – the world is coming round to the way that my generation wants to work. I'm proud of the fact that, while we prefer to keep our options open, we also want to be affluent and follow a clear career path. But I don't want to go down that path with just any company. I see myself as a socially responsible individual, not just in the views I hold or the products I buy, but in career terms as well. So, if a company has a really bad carbon footprint, or if the office environment is unwelcoming to specific people, I wouldn't want to work there, however good the salary might be.

Ⓑ ADAM

Businesses are always asking me how they can attract the best young candidates, and the first thing I tell them is: 'From the very first interview, don't just promote the positives of your company.' Unlike pretty much every generation before them, young adults today tend to avoid exaggerating their achievements when applying for a job. This, in my view, is a welcome development, but it also means that young adults expect nothing less than openness and integrity in return, and recruiters would do well to bear that in mind. It is also important to remember that the use of newspaper adverts and even generalised online noticeboards for both recruitment and job-seeking is becoming a thing of the past. Younger people now inhabit the world of social media, and companies wanting to attract dynamic employees in their early twenties should aim to produce targeted campaigns in that sphere. The businesses that have done this are already seeing the benefits, as reflected in the quality of the people coming to work for them.

Ⓒ FELIX

It's not surprising that young people suffer from anxiety about their careers. Our education system is increasingly focused on students achieving higher grades in a smaller range of subjects. The pressures they face are greater than ever before and their parents, while trying to prepare their children for an unstable job market and an uncertain future, often add to this stress without meaning to do so. So, when recent graduates sometimes make hopeful, even idealistic, demands on their new employer in certain areas such as social responsibility, it is easy to see why they do so, given the high standards they have become used to. They also have to deal with the misleading stereotype of people their age insisting on flexible working so they can be paid to sit around at home, doing nothing. While it is true that they often believe they should be allowed to work on their laptops at home, they rarely – if ever – do so without a clear understanding of what their role is and where their career is going next.

Ⓓ CORINNA

When I was growing up, my parents would always tell me to 'study hard, because there are no jobs out there.' I could never understand why they used to say that, as they would then disappear and go to work for twelve hours. They certainly helped me to grasp the value of hard work, but neither of them was truly happy in their boring office jobs. I decided that I wanted a career I can love, not just a high income, and part of that comes from collaboration. Today more than ever, it's vitally important to have the right network of contacts and my connections have been essential in growing my businesses. Technology is a huge part of what holds us together; mentally, I've always got about ten 'tabs' open in my mind, which helps me to keep track of what's going on each day in each of my companies. I can't say that I ever really switch off from work, but then not many people my age probably can.

GRAMMAR
WISH AND IF ONLY

1 Match the sentences.

1 He's going to miss his flight.
2 She can't concentrate in the office.
3 I'm feeling a bit sick.
4 We enjoyed our holiday so much.
5 His laptop has broken again.
6 She failed her exams.
7 Our new teacher is really good at explaining things.
8 My dad's just upset the neighbours again.

a He wishes he had the money to buy a new one.
b If only he'd got up earlier.
c I wish I hadn't eaten so much chocolate.
d I wish we were still there.
e If only people would be quiet.
f I wish she wouldn't keep forgetting my name, though.
g If only she had listened more in class.
h I wish he wasn't so rude all the time.

| 1 .... | 3 .... | 5 .... | 7 .... |
| 2 .... | 4 .... | 6 .... | 8 .... |

2 Which of the sentences a–h in Exercise 1:

1 talk about something we would like to be different in the present or future? ....
2 express regret about the past? ....
3 talk about something that's annoying that we want to change? ....

3 Complete the sentences with words in the box in the correct form.

> ~~be / warmer~~   have / more time
> know / the answer   listen / to you
> live / closer to them   order / a burger
> turn down / the music

0 I got really cold when I went out this morning.
  If only *it had been warmer*.
1 I don't think I'm going to finish my homework this evening. I wish ....
2 I can't solve this last crossword clue. If only I ....
3 It's really difficult to concentrate. I wish my brother ....
4 I don't really want this sandwich now. I wish I ....
5 I really miss seeing my family every day. I wish I ....
6 You were right – that restaurant was terrible. If only I ....

4 Choose the correct options.

1 If only it *had been / was* easy to write a CV!
2 I wish my interview *went / had gone* a little better.
3 I wish we *came / hadn't come* to work by bus today – it was so hot on board.
4 If only people *weren't / aren't* expected to work five days a week.
5 Do you sometimes wish you *hadn't applied / didn't apply* for this job?
6 I wish my boss *will / would* give me a promotion soon.

5 Correct the mistakes in the sentences or put a tick by any you think are correct.

1 If only I wouldn't work on Friday and Saturday evenings. ....
2 It's clear that you're keen to make a good impression, but I wish you calmed down a little. ....
3 The CEO only seems to promote people he socialises with. If only there wasn't a glass ceiling. ....
4 We're due to get a nice bonus this month, but if only we hit our sales targets. ....
5 I wish we could have worked together when we were younger. ....
6 I like to go shopping, but if only I have money. ....
7 If I only could travel back in time. I would tell my younger self to save more money. ....
8 If only they speak another language, they'd find travelling much easier. ....

6 Complete the sentences with the verbs in brackets in the correct form.

0 Sami wishes he *hadn't acted* (act) so rudely. He knows he upset you.
1 If only you .... (tell) me when you arrange your meetings.
2 I've got so much work to do – I wish I .... (know) where to start.
3 I wish it .... (rain) so heavily this morning – my suit is ruined.
4 Look, I can't help you with your essay. I wish you .... (keep) asking.
5 I wish I .... (learn) to say 'no' to people when I was younger.
6 I wish the day .... (end) soon. It's been one disaster after another.

7 Complete the table so that sentences A and B mean the same.

	A	B
0	It is so difficult to reply to all the emails I get each day.	I wish *it wasn't so difficult* to reply to all the emails I get each day.
1	I don't get paid enough for all the work I do.	If only .... for all the work I do.
2	Please stop tapping your fingers on the table – it's so annoying.	I wish .... your fingers on the table – it's so annoying.
3	Gabriela would love to be able to get her dream job.	Gabriela wishes .... get her dream job.
4	I'm really annoyed that I missed the train this morning.	If only .... missed the train this morning.
5	It would really make me happy to have 48 hours in a day.	I wish .... 48 hours in a day.
6	Apparently, Peter's training session was great. What a shame we missed it.	If only we .... Peter's training session.

48   **UNIT 8**

VOCABULARY
MONEY: IDIOMS AND PHRASAL VERBS

1 Match the words to make phrasal verbs for talking about money.

1 come	**a** around
2 come	**b** aside
3 get	**c** by on
4 put	**d** down
5 share	**e** into
6 shop	**f** off
7 splash	**g** out
8 rip (someone)	**h** out

1	**3**	**5**	**7** ....
2	**4**	**6**	**8** ....

2 Choose the correct options.

1 It's amazing how much the price of smart TVs has *come down / come into* over the past few years.

2 At the end of each month, I always make sure to *put aside / get by on* 5% of my wages. I'm saving to buy an apartment.

3 Some people buy the first thing they see, while others prefer to *share out / shop around* to make sure they get the best deal.

4 After her great-grandmother passed away, she *came down / came into* a huge inheritance.

5 Before she died, she *shopped around / shared out* her property between her children and grandchildren.

6 I've been given some money for my birthday, so I'm going to the mall to *rip off / splash out* on some new clothes.

7 David has found it easier to *get by on / put aside* his salary now he's stopped buying so many expensive clothes.

8 That jewellery shop on the high street is well known for *splashing out / ripping off* their customers.

3 Complete the sentences with the phrasal verbs from Exercise 1 in the correct form.

1 I really like that top, but it's so expensive. I'll wait until it has .... in price in the sales.

2 Paco .... a huge amount of money after he sold his business to a multinational company.

3 After Daniela's husband lost his job, they found it difficult to .... her salary alone.

4 The company plans to .... the £1.5 billion profit between its investors.

5 My sister never buys anything immediately. She's always .... for the best deals.

6 After getting good grades in her exams, Lucia rewarded herself by .... on a new smartphone.

7 It's becoming increasingly difficult for people to .... enough money for their retirement.

8 Did you really pay £3,000 for that awful car? They totally .... you .... !

4 Correct the mistakes in the idioms.

1 It's unbelievable how much I pay in tax. It's **daytime robbery**. ....

2 When I was growing up, we found it hard to **make ends match**. ....

3 That only costs £15, so it won't **hurt the bank**. ....

4 Everyone loves to hear a success story in which someone goes from **rags to rich**. ....

5 Those 2 for 1 offers in supermarkets are a **fake economy** because you end up paying for two things when you only actually need one. ....

6 I pay for a gym membership but never go – I'm **sending money down the sink**. ....

5 Complete the sentences with the correct idiom from Exercise 4.

1 After a poor start to life, Camila Alves went from .... and is now a hugely successful businessperson.

2 It'll be like pouring .... if you buy that coat – you'll only wear it once.

3 Even though my cousin says he finds it hard to ...., he buys a new pair of trainers every fortnight.

4 It won't .... to eat at that restaurant – it's far less expensive than you'd expect.

5 I couldn't believe how much my meal cost – it was .... ! I didn't even enjoy it!

6 Paying as little as possible for a laptop is a .... as you'll need to replace it with a new one soon enough.

6 Answer the questions so that they are true for you.

1 What do you like to splash out on?

2 What do you put money aside for?

3 What do you shop around for?

4 Can you think of anyone who has gone from rags to riches?

5 Have you ever paid too much for something and been ripped off?

6 What is the minimum amount of money that you could get by on each week?

WRITING
A FORMAL LETTER OR EMAIL

>> SEE *PREPARE TO WRITE* BOX, STUDENT'S BOOK PAGE 63

1 What should you include when writing an email of application? Circle *Yes* or *No*.

1	text speak (e.g. *lol*)	Yes / No
2	examples of relevant experience	Yes / No
3	exclamation marks	Yes / No
4	details of your daily schedule	Yes / No
5	a request for an interview	Yes / No
6	bullet points	Yes / No
7	extremely formal language	Yes / No
8	neutral/semi-formal language	Yes / No
9	a response to all points in the question	Yes / No

2 Complete the sentences with the words in the box.

> academic   background   contact
> employment   personal   qualifications

1 We can see that you've got an impressive educational _____ with a degree and Masters from the University of Cambridge.

2 If you could give us your _____ information, such as date of birth and address, we can set you up in the system.

3 I can't see anything in your CV relating to your _____ history. Have you had a full time job before?

4 If you leave your _____ details – an email and a phone number – we'll be in touch about organising an interview.

5 Tell us something about your _____ achievements. You graduated last year, didn't you?

6 In the application form, please include the details of any _____ gained, such as degrees, diplomas or any other titles relevant to the position.

3 Choose the best options for a formal letter or email.

1 I have *got / gained* relevant experience in a number of part-time roles.

2 I am hoping to *start / launch* my career in journalism at your organisation.

3 While I was at school, I spent time *supervising / looking after* younger students.

4 I have recently *done / completed* my football coaching badge, level 2.

5 I hope that my application has *shown / demonstrated* my suitability for the role.

6 Being a keen athlete, I *appreciate / know* the importance of self-discipline.

7 The teachers ran after school clubs for the younger students and I often *helped / assisted* them.

8 In July, I *was awarded / got* a first-class degree in computer science.

9 Working with children greatly *improved / enhanced* my understanding of the importance of interpersonal relationships.

10 I am confident that I *perform / do* well under pressure.

4 The words in bold are in the wrong sentence. Change their positions so that all the sentences are correct.

1 I believe that I am able to perform well under **skills**. _____

2 I would describe myself as outgoing, with a good sense of **sales**. _____

3 My three years' experience of working in **pressure** would be an advantage in this role. _____

4 As well as working well alone, I am also a strong team **attitude**. _____

5 I would bring excellent communication **humour** to the role. _____

6 I see the role as demanding a *can-do* **player**, and this is something I definitely have. _____

5 Look at the pictures. What qualities might a person need to work in these positions?

6 Read the question and make notes in the box underneath.

> *You see this post on your college message board:*
>
> **Work experience at a 4-star hotel in the capital**
> During the peak summer season, we will be offering two work experience places to college students in the local area. You will be working either on the reception desk (dealing with guests and their enquiries) or in the restaurant (assisting the waiting staff during the dinner service). Please let us know which type of role you would prefer, what experience or skills you have that are relevant to the job and how this opportunity would benefit you in the future.
> Carla Enoki

Role I'd be interested in:	
Relevant experience/skills:	
Benefit to me in the future:	

7 Read Susanna's email quickly. Has she fully addressed the task?

Dear Ms Enoki,

I am writing in response to the advert you posted on our college message board [1] about students coming to help out in your hotel. I would like to [2] let you know that I'm interested in the restaurant role.

For the past three years, I have worked part-time at a small local restaurant. I have experience working as a member of the waiting staff and occasionally as the host, [3] letting people come in and taking them to the right place. Furthermore, I have strong communication skills, being fluent in both Spanish and English, and have a competent level of Russian having completed a home-study course earlier this year. Your hotel, as I see from your website, is noticeably popular with Russian tourists and I would [4] love to be able to chat to them during the placement.

I am confident in my ability to work well under pressure, particularly when [5] talking to any customers who complain or expect too much. I feel that [6] these abilities would also work in your hotel's restaurant. Finally, my familiarity with our local cuisine would potentially be useful when [7] answering questions from guests about the menu.

If I were offered a placement, it would be a wonderful opportunity to [8] get better at working in hotels, restaurants, anywhere like that. Additionally, I am in the process of completing my university application, so, not only would this work experience improve my personal statement, it would also be particularly relevant as I am applying for a degree in tourism and hospitality management.

I hope to hear from you soon,

Susanna

8 Improve the email by replacing 1–8 with the phrases A–H.

A managing customer complaints and requests ....
B add to my skill set in the hospitality industry ....
C both of these skills are transferable to ....
D put myself forward for ....
E regarding potential work experience opportunities ....
F welcome the opportunity to interact with ....
G responding to enquiries ....
H welcoming guests and showing them to their tables ....

9 Complete the sentences, using the phrases in Exercise 8 as reference.

1 The course I did in client behaviour was difficult, but it certainly enabled me to add to my s_____ s_____.
2 Please wait. A customer service agent will r_____ to your e_____ shortly.
3 No one else wanted to lead the team, so I decided to p_____ myself f_____.
4 I am writing to you regarding p_____ work experience o_____ at your company.
5 The staff welcomed the o_____ to i_____ with the new CEO at the annual meeting.
6 The only approach to managing c_____ c_____ is to smile and apologise.
7 I have a positive and friendly personality, which I feel would be appreciated when welcoming g_____ to the hotel.
8 If you work in hospitality, you will develop s_____ that are t_____ to other jobs.

10 Read the question. Write your answer in 220–260 words.

You see this advertisement on a local message board:

Work experience at an IT business conference
We are offering work experience for young people to help out at a conference for international IT businesses. We're looking for friendly, mature young people with good skills in both languages and working as part of a team.
There are two areas in which we have vacancies. Firstly, at the conference centre entrance, where you will welcome visitors and offer them tea or coffee, and secondly, inside the conference hall itself, where you will provide customer service, such as communicating information about the times and locations of the different presentations. Please let us know which type of role you would prefer, what experience or skills you have that are relevant to the placement and how this opportunity would benefit you in the future.

Write your **email**.

VOCABULARY AND READING
EDUCATION

1 Complete the crossword, using the clues to help you.

Across

2 the process of thinking carefully about a subject or idea, without allowing feelings or opinions to affect you

3 the way that you progress in your work, either in one job or in a series of jobs

6 .... skills are the skills we use every day to interact and communicate with others

7 the activity of meeting people who might be useful to know, especially in your job

8 the set of characteristics that make a good leader

9 an amount of money given by a school, college, university or other organisation to pay for the studies of a person with great ability but little money

Down

1 a person who is learning or practising the skills of a particular job

2 suggestions and guidance about what jobs you could or should do

4 things that you hope to achieve in your life or career

5 a period of time working for a company or organisation in order to get experience of a particular type of work

2 Complete the sentences with the answers from Exercise 1.

1 Studying abroad is a great way to improve your ...., since you spend so much time meeting new people and developing relationships.

2 I can't afford to study abroad, but I'm really hoping that by working extra hard, I'll get a ....

3 I've always had .... of becoming a journalist.

4 These days, getting a new job is as much about .... as it is having the right skills.

5 Most of my family are teachers, but I'm determined to take a different ....

6 If you want to learn on the job and pick up new skills in the early stages of your career, there are many .... positions that you could apply for.

7 The most important piece of .... I was given at school was to do something I truly enjoy.

8 I often see *problem solving* listed on job descriptions, which is probably why it is so important to develop .... skills.

9 Doing an .... during the summer holidays really helped me to understand what kind of job I would like to do when I graduate.

10 I believe that the one thing school can't teach you is .... – people are either inspired by you, or they aren't.

3 Make notes to the following questions.

1 How important are good handwriting skills?

2 Do you think writing by hand will soon disappear? Why? / Why not?

4 Read the article on the opposite page quickly and compare your answers from Exercise 3 with the writer's ideas.

5 Read the article again and answer the questions.

In which paragraph does the writer:

1 justify a process that improves the recall of information?

2 mention how existing records of study can be easily modified?

3 refer to a point raised by medical specialists?

4 suggest that technology can lead to problems in maintaining focus?

5 make a specific reference to a particular analytical skill?

6 encourage the use of technology to ensure all students are supported?

THE END OF ACHING WRISTS?

A Over the past few years, it seems that writing by hand is quickly becoming less and less valued as a skill. As work and methods of study have been changed by technology over the past few decades, and every application for a course or scholarship is now submitted online, it might seem obvious that pens and pencils have become obsolete in the modern school or college. But is this actually progress? Not according to paediatricians who have expressed concerns about the fact that many children today find it difficult even to hold a pencil, thanks to their overuse of technology. Perhaps we have all underestimated the influence that handwriting has on learning and development.

B There have been a huge number of studies that show how writing by hand provides stimulation for certain parts of the brain. It creates a visual and sensual connection to the brain, which is less pronounced when writing on a computer, and enables learning to occur in a wide range of ways. How do you know what a word actually means until you've physically written it with your hand? There is also the proven connection that shows how memory can function best when physical activity or visual stimulation (or both) are involved. This is why primary-age children are encouraged to use sticks to draw in sand or rice.

C Developing handwriting skills also appears to be particularly crucial for children and teenagers in their cognitive development – the area of learning that focuses on language learning, conceptual understanding and information processing. This might actually be the most important point of all – that engaging with study material through handwriting allows for a deeper level of processing to occur. It far outweighs typing in that it enables students to reflect on the fundamental concepts in the material and to activate their critical thinking and questioning abilities.

D This is particularly relevant when it comes to note-taking. In the case of, say, taking notes in a lecture at university, students today often favour a laptop to a pen. But, by doing this, they become more likely to try and copy what the speaker is saying, word-for-word, and as a result fail to engage with the content in anything other than a superficial way. There is also the added risk that comes with having a laptop open – distraction. Important content during a lecture is often omitted by students who 'just have a quick look' on their social media pages.

E So, should we quit using laptops and return to pens? Not necessarily; not if we have aspirations of our classrooms becoming more inclusive than ever. For example, if a child has problems in developing their handwriting skills, forcing them to pick up a pencil can often do them more harm than good. They can lose confidence in their ability to express what they want to say or to complete their work as well as they know they can. And for those with additional learning difficulties such as dyslexia, who may be worried about displaying the difficulties they are having with writing to classmates, typing should allow them a way to manage this. It can also help those students from another language background to create better opportunities for communication with classmates.

F There are certainly times when writing by hand is simply impractical, the main issue being that manual notes take longer to put down on a page. What happens if you can't write fast enough to keep up with what the speaker is saying? What happens if your hand gets tired because, as mentioned earlier, people are not used to holding and writing with pens anymore? Also, with typed notes, you can more easily go back and edit them and you will probably have immediate access to a backup copy on the cloud.

G Ideally, a balance needs to be found. Writing and taking notes by hand is far more preferable for learning on a deeper level and for our memories, while using computers and tablets seems to be the better option for learning facts, for record-keeping during longer lectures, or for children and teenagers with handwriting issues. But, ultimately, despite the continual march of technology, you should not give up your pens and pencils just yet.

6 Match the **highlighted** words in the article to the meanings.

1 aiming to include many different types of people and treat them all fairly and equally _____

2 ignored or not included _____

3 happening repeatedly _____

4 be greater or more important than something else _____

5 easily noticeable; obvious; certain _____

GRAMMAR
CLEFT SENTENCES

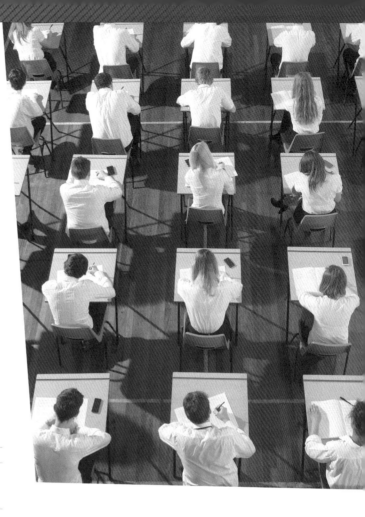

1 Match the sentence halves.

1 It was when I was in primary school
2 What he needs to understand is
3 It is just after I've eaten lunch
4 It was my eldest brother
5 What you need to do to pass this exam is
6 What I hoped for was

a make sure you revise twice a week.
b to get high grades in all my subjects.
c that I first met my best friend.
d that I find it most difficult to study.
e that I can't always help him with his homework.
f who taught me how to play the piano.

1	3	5 ....
2	4	6 ....

2 Change the cleft sentences into non-cleft sentences.

1 What is important in a university application is attention to detail.

....

2 What he suddenly realised was that he had missed an entire page of questions in the test.

....

3 It wasn't until May when I realised that I wanted to take a gap year.

....

4 It is my current English teacher whose lessons I find most helpful.

....

5 What I needed was to go home when I started to feel ill.

....

6 If we don't know the answer, what we should do is ask the teacher for help.

....

3 Rewrite the non-cleft sentences as cleft sentences, starting with the word in brackets.

1 I would love to finish my homework on time this week. (What)

....

2 Taking effective notes in class will help you write better essays. (It)

....

3 Gerard is hoping to go to Pompeu Fabra University next year. (What)

....

4 I'll be disappointed if I don't meet all of my university offers. (What)

....

5 I was surprised by the complexity of her argument. (It)

....

6 Thinking about the next day's classes keeps me awake at night. (What)

....

7 I'm concerned about your lack of effort. (It)

....

8 Some people can memorise everything they read and I find that amazing. (What)

....

4 Correct the mistakes in the sentences or put a tick by any you think are correct.

1 It was me who wanted to study English abroad.

....

2 It was her that originally encouraged me to read more widely. ....

3 What I enjoyed most about college was the friendships I developed. ....

4 What we need more than anything have a separate room for private study. ....

5 It was that she was visiting as a tourist that she realised she wanted to study in Milan. ....

6 What you need to do is setting aside an extra hour at the weekend for revision. ....

VOCABULARY
EDUCATION: PHRASAL VERBS

1 Match the sentence halves.

1 In my country, state schools break
2 Many students find it difficult to catch
3 Jaime's really unhappy at the moment and is considering dropping
4 Our teacher's been off for a month – we're all going to fall
5 Work hard at the start of the year and you'll get
6 At the end of every class, my teachers quickly go
7 I'm so stressed! By the end of this week I've got to hand
8 Before I go to university, I'm going to read

a up if they join a new school late in the year.
b in about ten pieces of homework!
c behind if we don't get extra lessons.
d up for summer in June.
e out of college altogether.
f up on the way degree-level work gets assessed.
g through the end of year exams more easily.
h over what we've been learning, which helps a lot.

1		3		5		7	
2		4		6		8	

2 Complete the conversation with the phrasal verbs from Exercise 1 in the correct form.

A: I've not managed to ¹ _____ my science homework yet, have you?
B: No chance. I was off last week, remember? I've not even ² _____ on everything I missed in class yet.
A: Oh, yeah, of course you were. If you like, I can ³ _____ it with you.
B: That'd be amazing,
A: You'll probably have to ⁴ _____ some of the ideas that I can't explain too clearly afterwards, though.
B: That's fine, anything will help. I'm just concerned about ⁵ _____ .
A: Don't worry, you won't.
B: I'm not sure. I can't believe how much harder it's been in the final year. I feel like ⁶ _____ sometimes.
A: That's crazy! What would you do then?
B: Nothing, probably. Ah, you're right. We just need to ⁷ _____ our final exams.
A: Exactly. Just wait until we've done them all and ⁸ _____ for the summer. You'll feel differently then.

EDUCATION: VERB AND NOUN COLLOCATIONS

3 Complete the table with correct collocations using the nouns in the box.

> a dream   a goal (x2)   a visit   an application
> an understanding   fees   high standards   requirements

gain	fulfil	pay	set	submit

4 Complete the advert with the correct verb and noun collocations from Exercise 3.

Are you the type of person who ¹ _____ high standards for themselves? Do you want to fulfil a long-term ² _____ and become successful in your chosen career?

Our company provides one-to-one, private tuition for students who are preparing for their final exams and aiming to ³ _____ the requirements of the university course they are applying for. And the best part? We are giving away 20 hours' worth of *free* online classes – there will be no fees to ⁴ _____ for successful applicants.

All you need to do is submit your online ⁵ _____ by this Saturday and we will contact you if you are successful.

5 Read the article below and decide which answer (A, B, C or D) best fits each gap.

Teachers were students, too

Whenever they believe they are being **(0)** *set* too much homework, students can start to act negatively towards their teacher. In return, that same teacher might get annoyed about students failing to **(1)** _____ it in on time, and this is when the lines of communication stop working.

It is vital to remember this: at some point, all teachers were students. Every teacher had their own goals to **(2)** _____ when they were a teenager. Even the brightest, most qualified teachers worried about falling **(3)** _____ in their studies and wondered how they would get **(4)** _____ their exams without the pressure becoming too much. They would even nervously **(5)** _____ an occasional visit to a careers advisor.

What can be done? Wherever possible, both sides should try to be more open in order to **(6)** _____ a better understanding of each other's concerns. Young people might ask their teachers what they were like at the same age. How did they cope with the workload? Which career **(7)** _____ did they follow to get to this point? Finding common ground is a social **(8)** _____ that cannot be valued highly enough.

0 A fixed	**B** arranged	**C** put	**Ⓓ** set
1 A hand	**B** submit	**C** show	**D** pass
2 A deliver	**B** fulfil	**C** perform	**D** complete
3 A away	**B** behind	**C** off	**D** down
4 A across	**B** by	**C** over	**D** through
5 A hold	**B** give	**C** pay	**D** lend
6 A increase	**B** win	**C** gain	**D** add
7 A path	**B** way	**C** avenue	**D** course
8 A technique	**B** method	**C** ability	**D** skill

LISTENING

1 You are going to listen to a girl and her cousin talking about the different schools they attend. Tick the things they mention.

	Girl	Boy
teachers		
classmates		
school uniform		
classroom study		

2 Listen to the girl again and complete the text with the words that you hear.

> My teachers must have been on a training course or something; they've been much more effective in
> ¹ _____ recently. There's also been a change to the timetable this year, and we've got one period each week where we sit down and discuss our studies with ² _____, without any teachers present. I'm certainly making the most of the chance to ³ _____ of other subjects, anyway. It ⁴ _____ from regular classes, which are always focused on the one thing.

3 Answer the question below.

1 Which aspect of attending her school does the girl enjoy?
  A the opportunity to explore new ideas
  B the atmosphere during lessons
  C the variety of teaching styles

4 Listen to the boy again. Make notes about what he says about the other students in his group in relation to:

- achieving high grades
- working during self-study periods
- encouraging each other

....

....

....

....

5 Read the question below. What is the correct answer?

2 What point is the boy making about other students in his year group?
  A They work more efficiently during self-study periods.
  B They encourage each other in their academic progress.
  C They are intensely focused on achieving high grades.

6 You will hear two more extracts. For questions 3–6, choose the answer (A, B or C) which fits best according to what you hear. There are two questions for each extract.

Extract 2
You hear two teachers talking about homework.

3 What point does the man make about giving a deadline?
  A It motivates the students to complete homework early.
  B It provides weaker students with a sense of structure.
  C It ensures that school rules are followed correctly.

4 Why does the woman refer to the last homework she set?
  A to illustrate how teenagers think differently to adults
  B to show how setting target dates can be restricting
  C to demonstrate the value of keeping to a schedule

Extract 3
You hear two first-year university students discussing their studies.

5 How did the man feel at the start of his course?
  A confident that it will inspire him to get good grades
  B surprised at how much further reading he needs to do
  C reassured that the materials are designed for independent learning

6 What do they agree was missing from their high school education?
  A practice in the study skills needed at degree level
  B preparation for the seminar format of teaching
  C tuition in planning and writing academic essays

1 Look at Exercise 5. What do you think the title could mean? Read the article quickly to check your ideas, ignoring the gaps.

2 Look at Exercise 5 again. The example (0) is given. Are any of the following words possible as an alternative answer?

A over
B out
C back

3 Which of the following are *not* possible for question (1)?

A are
B stayed
C were
D felt
E will be

4 Why are the following answers to question (2) incorrect?

A off
B away
C back
D behind others

5 For questions 1–8, read the text below and think of the word which best fits the gap. Only use one word in each gap.

My online helper

In the old days, catching (0) _*up*_ on missed schoolwork often meant borrowing a friend's book and copying what they had written down in class. If you (1) _____ lucky, you might have had a friend who would be able to go through their work with you, and you could avoid falling too far (2) _____. More frequently, however, students would simply borrow a friend's book and copy down pages of words or numbers with (3) _____ or no help or explanation from the teacher.

We are so much luckier today. Rather than all the music videos or latest games cheats, (4) _____ often attracts young people to YouTube and similar sites is the wealth of information you can find and (5) _____ an understanding of. This is particularly relevant (6) _____ catching up on missed classes – someone, somewhere, (7) _____ already have posted a video to help you out.

My parents still worry about me being online. But, as important as it is to emphasise online safety, there's no reason to feel hostile (8) _____ the internet. It's such a valuable learning tool.

6 Read the article in Exercise 9 quickly, ignoring the gaps. What is the writer's purpose?

A to explain how to apply to university
B to tell an amusing anecdote from her past
C to criticise people who come across as arrogant

7 Why are the following answers incorrect for the example (0)?

A admit
B admiration
C admission

8 Which of the options is correct and why?

I was helping to process *applicants / applications* for the following academic year.

9 For questions 1–8, read the text below. Use the word given in capitals at the end of some of the lines to form a word that fits in the gap in the same line.

THE PERSONAL STATEMENT EXPERIENCE

I did some work experience in a university	
(0) _admissions_ office during my gap year,	ADMIT
helping to process (1) _____	APPLY
for the following academic year. In the	
UK, these have to include a personal	
statement, and I was lucky enough to have	
the opportunity to read the unintentionally	
entertaining words supporting the	
(2) _____ of college students.	ASPIRE
One particularly confident person had	
written: 'I display my considerable	
(3) _____ skills every day just	LEAD
by being me.' Someone else claimed	
that he would love the chance to show	
how (4) _____ he was, and	KNOW
challenged the faculty professor to an	
online quiz. I remember shaking my head	
while reading that one. There was another	
who, (5) _____, thought that it	APPEAR
would help her cause to include an extra	
(6) _____ and attached an image	SUBMIT
file of herself meeting Michelle Obama.	
I sometimes found it a real test	
of (7) _____ doing that job. But	ENDURE
I got a great sense of (8) _____	FULFIL
out of knowing how good, in comparison,	
my own personal statement had been.	

10 CRIME AND PUNISHMENT

VOCABULARY AND READING
PUNISHMENT FOR CRIME

1 Match the verbs with the phrases.

0 arrested		**a** with a crime
1 found		**b** for a crime
2 issued		**c** to six years in prison
3 charged		**d** on suspicion of burglary
4 pay		**e** with a fine
5 plead		**f** guilty of theft
6 prosecuted		**g** guilty to a crime
7 report		**h** damages to somebody
8 sentenced		**i** someone to the police

0	_d_	**2**	....	**4**	....	**6**	....	**8**	....
1	....	**3**	....	**5**	....	**7**	....		

2 Complete the news report with words from Exercise 1.

THE BATMAN BURGLAR

Alex Williams, known locally as *The Batman Burglar* because of the superhero costume he wore when out committing his crimes, won't be causing any more misery in the town where he lives.

Williams was first [1] _____ to the police by his sister, whose house he would always return to after a night of burglary. When the police arrived at the scene, they found him still in full costume, sitting on the roof of his sister's house, and ordered him to come down immediately. Williams jumped from the roof onto a police officer's back, injuring her in the process. He was [2] _____ on _____ of burglary. Once they got to the police station, they also [3] _____ him with causing injury to a police officer.

In court, where Williams was later taken to be [4] _____ for his crimes, he decided, against the advice of his lawyer, to [5] _____ not _____ to either of the charges. Unsurprisingly, it took the jury less than twenty minutes of discussion to [6] _____ him _____.
The judge had little sympathy for Williams' tears as he begged to be set free and he was ordered to [7] _____ of £1,000 to each of his victims, as well as being [8] _____ with a _____ of £500 for damaging his sister's roof. He was [9] _____ to three months in _____ for injuring the police officer.

3 Read the title and first sentence of the article on the opposite page. Do you think the writer will be:

A generally sympathetic towards young cybercriminals?
B generally critical of young cybercriminals?
C both critical and sympathetic?

4 Read the rest of the article quickly and check your answer.

5 Read the article again. For questions 1–6, choose the answer (A, B, C or D) which you think fits best according to the text.

1 What does the writer suggest about Jack in the second paragraph?
A He has lost contact with many people since his time as a cybercriminal.
B He understands how damaging certain aspects of his life were.
C He regrets taking so many photographs of himself and his friends.
D He became a cybercriminal to escape a job that he hated.

2 What does the writer state about cybercrime in the third paragraph?
A It relies on access to information about people's lifestyles.
B It involves fairly straightforward methods.
C It requires a high degree of intelligence to commit.
D It focuses primarily on people with wealth.

3 In the fourth paragraph, the writer describes the methods used by the cybercriminals as
A adapted to suit each individual who has been targeted.
B developed with some cooperation from businesses.
C applied with a thorough approach to each stage.
D designed to ensure that the crime is committed quickly.

4 Which phrase could correctly replace 'succumb to the lure of' in the fifth paragraph?
A feel tempted by
B understand the value of
C expect to make much
D spend a great deal of

5 What generalisation does the writer make about young hackers in the sixth paragraph?
A They are extremely skilled in the way they use their talents.
B They are sometimes not being truthful in their claims.
C They are interested in the chance to work with governments.
D They are desperate to move out of their parents' home.

6 What point does the writer make about online gaming websites in the last paragraph?
A They have been created to provide a safe space for younger gamers.
B People use them to connect with their schoolfriends online.
C They actively promote the misuse of programming technology.
D People exploit them in ways they were not intended to be used.

The honourable cause and the selfish instinct

Cybercrime and hacking is widespread, well-organised and, as journalist Stuart Armer finds out, is becoming increasingly appealing to young people who are eager to make money, impress their friends or even change the political system.

Unlike most teenagers who work in a bicycle shop, Jack was once able to post photos of himself and his friends being driven around central London in a limousine, dressed head to toe in designer clothes, holding thick rolls of cash. When I first meet him, even though he still has the pictures in his phone of this time he spent living the high life, he needs some persuading to show me them. Swiping his way from one image to the next, he turns silent, the significance of the situation still very much on his mind. The truth is, this lifestyle was only made possible through cyberfraud, a crime which, while relatively new to the world, comes increasingly with a huge financial and personal cost.

Cybercrime happens on such a wide and varied scale that it takes your breath away. In the UK in 2019, almost £200,000 per day was lost to cybercrime, a figure that doesn't even include the cost to banks and corporations. The approach is typically far less complex than one might imagine because, as Jack explains, 'it's all very well being clever, but you can't just rely on that. Getting lucky is what it's all about.' Potential victims will get spam emails or messages notifying them they've been caught breaking the speed limit or that they have an unexpected tax bill, for example. They haven't of course, but they are threatened with paying a huge fine or else face a prison sentence.

Once a person who agrees to pay has been found, they receive the hacker's bank account details and transfer the money. Jack's bosses had created a system to ensure that everything went according to plan. You might even admire the attention to detail if the whole process wasn't so shocking. 'We hacked their phone numbers as well as their online account details,' he explains. 'So that, at the exact moment their money was being transferred, if they suddenly changed their mind, we'd be constantly calling them, blocking the line. They wouldn't be able to get through to their bank.' By the time that person did manage to speak to someone, it was too late. Their money was gone.

This is not the full extent of cybercrime, however. A recent study by the National Crime Agency (NCA) concluded that, on the whole, the average young hacker does not succumb to the lure of money. While conducting interviews with teenagers who had committed computer-based crimes, the NCA found that most are entirely happy to be pulled in another direction, fixated on other purposes. They much prefer hacking companies in order to force them to address technical issues with website design or functionality, or showing off to their friends that they have the skills to be able to get inside supposedly secure web systems.

Some young hackers view their activities in the context of an uncompromising mission, declaring an ambition to draw attention to the inequalities in the world. There have been many examples of government infrastructure being attacked, with the hackers aiming to force the authorities to change certain policies – whether national or international – for the benefit of everyone. In one way, their sense of morality puts Jack and his activities to shame. Yet it is difficult not to wonder whether their true aim might actually be to launch themselves out of their bedrooms into a world where they are notorious for their work. The fact is, hackers at this high level are bound to get caught at some point and end up with their face across the news channels.

Admittedly, this might seem unfair, given that the career of the cybercriminal most often begins in far more innocent surroundings. They join websites dedicated to their favourite online games, finding valuable social interaction and support in forums. 'When I joined those sites, it was like I'd made some true friendships,' admits Jack. These message boards are full of tips, hints and, crucially, cheats which users avidly share with each other. As the NCA has found, creating cheats for games is a widespread practice that gives people the chance to develop their skills in coding and developing malware, and allows them to showcase these skills to their peers. Or that's the idea, in any case. In reality, large numbers of users are older, experienced cybercriminals who log on pretending to be like-minded teenagers and use the message boards as places to attract new personnel. People like Jack, keeping quiet and working in a bike shop, are grateful that he has been given a second chance.

6 Match the highlighted words in the article to the meanings.

1 fixed and not changing, especially when faced with opposition _____

2 deal with a problem _____

3 in an extremely keen or interested way _____

4 existing or happening in many places and/or among many people _____

5 unfair situations in which some people have more opportunities than others _____

GRAMMAR
INVERSION

1 Rearrange the words in bold to form correct phrases.

1 **rude it only is not** to use bad language in some countries, but it is also against the law.

2 **should circumstances under ride you no** a motorbike without wearing a helmet.

3 **I would no commit way ever would** a crime unless I was completely desperate.

4 **do at late night not until** the most serious crimes take place.

5 **ever rarely to will minor offences lead** to an arrest, despite being reported to the police.

6 **only the police did know when I arrived** how serious the situation was.

7 **the thieves that realise did little** the police were waiting for them inside the bank.

8 **I would not one for moment** stay friends with someone if they committed a serious crime.

2 Complete the sentences with the words in the box.

> Little   No way   Not for one moment
> Not only   Not until   Only when
> Rarely   Under no circumstances

1 _____ are people allowed to take photographs in court.

2 _____ did I ever imagine that I'd end up studying law at university.

3 _____ the third year of the investigation were the police convinced their evidence was sufficient to bring charges.

4 _____ is it difficult to believe your story, there is also a witness who can prove it isn't true.

5 _____ did Rico realise at the time that he was being filmed by a hidden security camera.

6 _____ did he deserve the sentence he received – it was his first offence!

7 _____ a prisoner is ready to join society again should they be released.

8 _____ do people turn to crime unless they feel they have no other choice.

3 Correct the mistakes in the sentences or put a tick by any you think are correct.

1 Not only there are prison sentences that are too short, but also others which are too long.

2 In no circumstances could it be described as acceptable to graffiti a monument.

3 Never before I slept so well as the night I was released from jail.

4 Never had they enjoyed a two-week period as much as their jury service.

4 Rewrite the sentences so that the meaning is the same.

1 There's no way the police will find whoever is guilty of this crime.
No way _____.

2 I won't rest until we've explored every part of this investigation.
Not until _____.

3 No one should be forced to hand over their personal details under any circumstances.
Under no circumstances _____.

4 People rarely worry about crime when they are on holiday.
Rarely _____.

5 The lawyer was exhausted. Also, he had started to doubt his client's story.
Not only _____.

6 I only understood how complex a police investigation can be after I had seen a documentary on TV.
Only after _____.

5 Complete the sentences using inversion and the verb in brackets.

0 When she was first arrested, little _did she realise_ that this would be the first of many appearances in a police interview room. (realise)

1 Cybercrime is a huge concern to the authorities because, not only _____ more common, it is also incredibly difficult to stop. (become)

2 When he got up that morning, no way _____ to find a mysterious deposit of £1 million in his bank account. (expect)

3 If someone is arrested, under no circumstances _____ to be interviewed without a lawyer. (agree)

4 Not until he lost everything he had ever worked for _____ with people who had turned to a life of crime. (identify)

5 Only when I have fitted security cameras in every room of my house _____ safe from being burgled. (feel)

6 Her detective training course was complete. Never _____ so much as in the six months she'd spent here. (learn)

CRIME AND PUNISHMENT: COLLOCATIONS AND SUFFIXES

1 Complete the crossword, using the clues to help you.

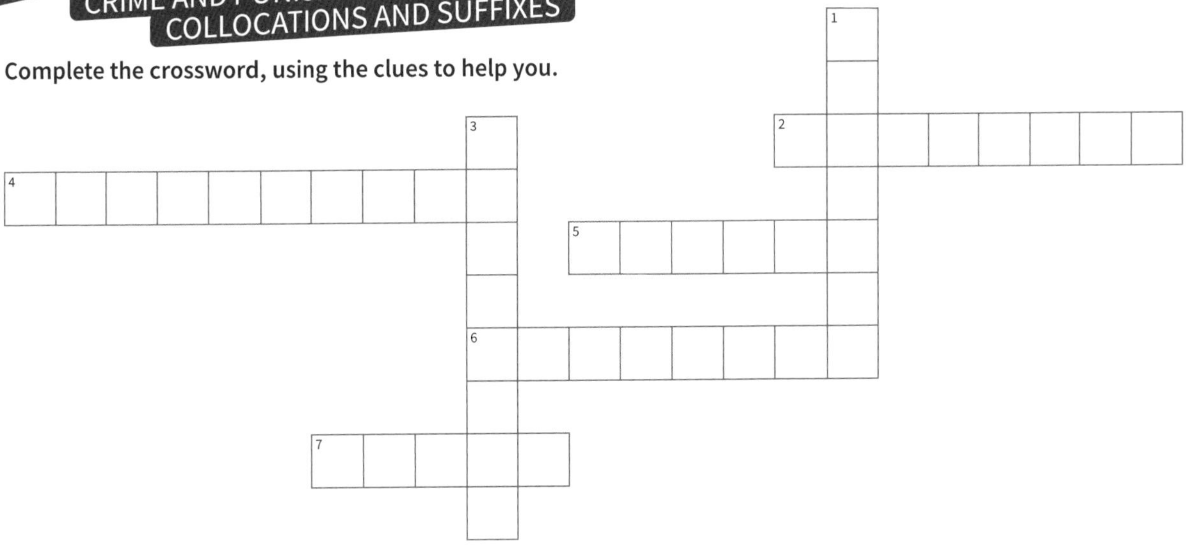

[Crossword grid with numbered cells 1-7]

Across

2 a person who commits a crime
4 a person who takes goods illegally from a shop without paying for them
5 a person who intentionally damages property belonging to other people
6 a person who is guilty of a crime
7 a person who steals things (not necessarily from private property)

Down

1 a person who illegally enters a building and steals things
3 a person who has been sent to jail as a punishment

2 Write the verb and noun forms of the words 1–7 from Exercise 1.

1 *burgle, burglary*   5 ....
2 ....   6 ....
3 ....   7 ....
4 ....

3 Correct the words in bold. It may be a spelling mistake or an incorrect collocation.

0 The judge ordered him to pay a fine and perform 100 hours of **communal service**.
   community service
1 15 months of his **imprisomment** was spent in the King County jail. ....
2 My cousin received a two-year **jail punishment** for stealing mobile phones. ....
3 **Arranged crime** remains one of the biggest threats to society. ....
4 Because of his young age, we're hoping he'll be given a **soft sentence.** ....
5 If a child commits a **minimum offence**, for example vandalism, the police will often just talk to the parents. ....
6 **Pretty theft** is when objects of a relatively low value are stolen. ....
7 Someone who commits the same crime more than once is known as a **repetitive offender.** ....
8 The schools in this area are often vulnerable to **vandelism.** ....

4 Complete the text with the corrected words or phrases from Exercise 3.

In an attempt to avoid overcrowding in prisons, which is becoming more common, judges often sentence offenders to ¹ .... Elsewhere, when there is no alternative to ² ...., human rights campaigners are keen to see more people given ³ .... when they have committed a ⁴ .... such as ⁵ ...., i.e. stealing something that has little value. This seems logical, as police and prosecutors could then focus their attention on ensuring that ⁶ .... and those involved in ⁷ .... are given ⁸ .... more appropriate to the level of distress they cause.

5 Choose the correct options. In some sentences, both are correct.

1 On the street where I live, rates of *burglary / crime* are higher than anywhere else in the city.
2 It could be argued that community *service / sentence* benefits the local area.
3 Jeffrey Skilling, former CEO of Enron, initially received a jail *punishment / sentence* of 24 years, but eventually served twelve.
4 My uncle was once falsely accused of *theft / burglary*, even though he hadn't been anywhere near the shopping centre that day.
5 The police are investigating how a valuable painting in the National Gallery was *vandalised / stolen* earlier this week.
6 The European Parliament estimates that organised *crime / punishment* costs the European economy somewhere between €218 and €282 billion each year.
7 In my opinion, people who commit *cruelty / crime* to animals should be put in prison.
8 The government should do more to ensure that *offenders / criminals* receive help after they leave prison.

WRITING
AN ESSAY

>> SEE *PREPARE TO WRITE* BOX, STUDENT'S BOOK PAGE 79

1 Look at the task and answer the questions.

> Your class has taken part in a discussion focusing on what leads young people to commit crimes
>
> > **Reasons why young people commit crime:**
> > - negative influence of peers
> > - lack of age-appropriate facilities in their area
> > - weak discipline from parents
> >
> > > **Some opinions expressed during the discussion:**
> > > 'A lot of young people do something illegal to show off to their friends.'
> > > 'There are hundreds of playgrounds for small kids, but nothing for teenagers to do.'
> > > 'You're more likely to commit crime if your parents let you get away with anything.'
>
> Write an essay discussing two of the reasons why young people commit crime. You should explain which has the greatest effect on teenagers' behaviour, giving reasons to support your answer.
> You may, if you wish, make use of the opinions expressed in the discussion, but you should use your own words as far as possible.

1 Which of the three reasons do you think is the easiest / most difficult to find valid ideas for?

2 Which two of the opinions expressed do you most agree with and why?

2 Which of the following sentences does not rephrase any of the opinions provided?

1 Young people often find themselves with little to do and, importantly, nowhere suitable to go in order to reduce the boredom they might feel.

2 It is common knowledge that teenagers get into trouble when they are left to find their own way in life, without being disciplined by their parents.

3 In some cases, the pressures of modern life can have a negative impact on young people and they might react in an extremely negative way.

4 As has always been the case, young people today seek approval from the people they associate with, often by breaking rules or even laws.

3 Read the answer to the task quickly. Do you think that the student has answered the question satisfactorily?

> It's generally true that young people do not set out to become offenders but rather [1] start committing crimes unintentionally. When this does happen, it is often due to a lack of positive role models to imitate, in both friends and family.
>
> Many people believe that, [2] in all cases, young people commit crime because their friends encourage them to and their motivation is, [3] above all, to gain respect and a higher status within their group. It is not surprising that this happens, given how important friendship networks are to kids, and many of them are so concerned with gaining approval that they find themselves in trouble with the authorities. They do not often consider the consequences of committing a crime and prefer the threat of being arrested to 'losing face' in front of their friends.
>
> A second argument suggests that the main problem comes from weak parenting. The absence of a strong role model at home [4] forces them to look somewhere else for [5] feeling important and accepted. Parents everywhere have a duty to educate their kids, but they should also ensure that he or she remains safe, which is not always the case. This often comes from creating a strong sense of discipline. Although people don't generally agree on the best way to bring up a [6] happy, reasonable, and confident person, there can be no denying that, if young people grow up feeling that they can get away with anything, life as a young offender [7] doesn't worry them much.
>
> Now that I have considered both sides, I have decided that there would be fewer crimes committed by young people if we could just ensure that all parents [8] take their responsibilities seriously. Unfortunately, this isn't an easy thing to do.

4 Use the checklist to confirm your answer to Exercise 3. Write *Yes* or *No*.

1 The first paragraph gives a relevant and appropriate introduction. ....

2 There is no informal language in the essay. ....

3 The candidate has used a range of vocabulary and grammar. ....

4 Each paragraph focuses on one topic. ....

5 In the conclusion, the candidate explains which reason they believe has the greatest effect. ....

6 The candidate only discusses two of the reasons given, not all three. ....

7 The candidate does not copy the words from the opinions but uses different words/phrases instead. ....

8 All ideas in the essay are relevant to the question. ....

9 The candidate has shown an ability to use a considerable range of natural, idiomatic language. ....

10 There is a wide variety of sentence structures. ....

5 Replace the highlighted phrases 1–8 in Exercise 3 with the idiomatic phrases A–H below.

A holds no great fear ....
B well-adjusted individual ....
C fall into a life of crime ....
D first and foremost ....
E drives them to look elsewhere ....
F without fail ....
G do not shy away from their responsibilities ....
H a sense of belonging ....

6 Rephrase the sentences using the words in the box.

> Having considered   hold the opinion
> issue   no wonder   probably fair to say
> there is no real consensus   widely believed

1 It is generally true It is	that young people do not start life with a plan to become offenders.
2 Many people believe It is .... Many people	that young people commit crime because their friends encourage them to.
3 It is not surprising It is	that this happens.
4 Although people don't generally agree Although	on the best way to bring up a child …
5 The main problem The main	comes from weak parenting.
6 Now that I have considered	both sides, I have decided that …

7 Rewrite the sentences using the grammatical structures provided.

1 Cleft sentence with *what*
The absence of a strong role model at home forces them to look somewhere else for a sense of belonging.
What ....

2 Inversion with *not only*
Parents have a duty to educate their child and they should also ensure that he or she remains safe.
Not only ....

3 Cleft sentence with *it*
Young people commit crime because their friends encourage them to.
It ....

4 Inversion with *rarely*
They do not often consider the consequences of committing a crime.
Rarely ....

5 *If only*
Unfortunately, this isn't an easy thing to do.
If only ....

6 2nd conditional
They are so concerned with gaining approval that they find themselves in trouble with the authorities.
If ....

8 Read the question. Write your answer in 220–260 words.

> Your class has taken part in a discussion focusing on what punishments should be made a priority to discourage teenagers from re-offending.
>
> **Potential punishments for teenagers who commit petty crimes:**
> • community service
> • young offenders' prisons
> • anti-crime support courses
>
> > **Some opinions expressed during the discussion:**
> > 'Petty criminals should help their local communities to compensate for their offences.'
> > 'If teenagers experience prison, there is more chance they will change their ways.'
> > 'Teenagers who are likely to re-offend need guidance and perhaps therapy to ensure they do not do so.'
>
> Write an essay discussing two of the potential methods of punishments that could be given to teenagers who commit petty crimes. You should explain which, in your opinion, might have the most success in discouraging re-offending, giving reasons to support your answer.
> You may, if you wish, make use of the opinions expressed in the discussion, but you should use your own words as far as possible.

VOCABULARY AND READING
DESCRIBING FOOD

1 Read the definitions and complete 1–10 with a word or phrase. The first letters have been given to help you.

0 chemicals used to stop food from decaying
1 containing a lot of, or too much, fat
2 food that is growing now and at its best
3 containing a large quantity of something
4 lacking a strong or particular flavour; not interesting
5 a meal that is unhealthy but is quick and easy to eat
6 containing a small quantity of something
7 grown without any artificial chemicals
8 food containing a large amount of oil, butter, eggs or cream
9 food or any other substance or material that is grown or obtained through farming
10 food prepared and bought at a shop but taken somewhere else, often home, to be heated and eaten

0 p *reservatives*
1 f
2 i   s
3 h   i
4 b
5 j   f
6 l   i
7 o
8 r
9 p
10 r   m

2 Complete the sentences with a word or phrase from Exercise 1 in the correct form.

1 To help tackle the obesity crisis, the government has passed a law banning all TV advertising of _____ after 8 pm.
2 My mum would never eat a strawberry in December – everything has to be completely _____ .
3 When I went to the UK, I ate some of the _____ food I have ever eaten – everything was so tasteless!
4 It's healthier to buy _____ food, but it is usually more expensive.
5 There's nothing wrong with putting a _____ in the microwave from time to time!
6 I do love a dessert at the end of a meal, but if it's too _____ , I usually can't finish it.
7 If you're looking for fresh local _____ , the Sunday market is absolutely amazing.
8 When food is _____ fat, it doesn't mean it's healthier. In fact, it's usually _____ sugar to make it taste better.
9 Foods which last longer have usually had _____ added to them.
10 Paz decided to become a vegetarian after she had a really _____ steak and felt ill for two days afterwards.

3 Choose the correct options.

1 While baked potatoes are healthy, chips and fries can be extremely *fatty / organic*, as they have been fried in oil.
2 It's easier to maintain a healthy diet if you avoid eating *junk food / produce*.
3 Supermarkets have recognised the increasing popularity of *organic / fatty* food.
4 Most people like eating chicken, but I find it can be a little bit *in season / bland*.
5 It might seem strange, but some fruits can actually be *rich in / high in* fat.
6 Following a vegan diet means avoiding meat and dairy *preservatives / produce*.

4 Read the first paragraph of the article on the opposite page, ignoring the gaps. Which sentence best summarises the main point of the article?

A People have a responsibility to become vegan or vegetarian.
B People are more accepting of non-meat diets in today's society.
C People tend to eat more healthily when they are younger.

5 Read the paragraph again. Decide which answer (A, B, C or D) best fits each gap.

0 A undertaken	**B** underdone	**C** undergone	**D** understood
1 A income	**B** revenue	**C** profits	**D** gains
2 A original	**B** different	**C** fresh	**D** new
3 A alert	**B** awake	**C** aware	**D** attentive
4 A interactions	**B** exchanges	**C** contacts	
D communications			
5 A adopting	**B** keeping	**C** including	**D** arranging
6 A impressions	**B** notions	**C** reflections	**D** intentions
7 A Apart	**B** Except	**C** Not	**D** Excluding
8 A available	**B** free	**C** set	**D** open

6 Read the rest of the article and answer the questions. Write *Sara*, *Dasha* or *both*.

Which person
1 relates their beliefs to childhood experience? _____
2 expresses pride in the actions of other people from their country? _____
3 states that their national dishes rely heavily on animal produce? _____
4 explains that their lifestyle choice is primarily for moral reasons? _____
5 suggests a reason for an established belief in society? _____
6 supports their argument with statistics? _____
7 mentions a sense of relief at not having to justify their diet to others? _____
8 indicates that their tastes have not changed since becoming a vegetarian? _____

THE MODERN PASSION FOR
Veganism and Vegetarianism

The world of food and healthy eating has **(0)** _undergone_ huge changes since the start of the 21st century. As today's young people move into adulthood and get jobs, they are keen to spend their **(1)** .... in ways that they feel comfortable with. Healthy and principled approaches to life are nothing **(2)** ...., but there is no doubt that populations across the globe are becoming increasingly **(3)** .... of the world around us and how all of our **(4)** .... with the environment have consequences. What's more, in today's society, it is uncommon for people to tease or mock you for being a vegan or vegetarian. Society is moving towards **(5)** .... a state of tolerance that is much improved compared to the outdated **(6)** .... of the past, and we seem to be creating a world in which all tastes and preferences are welcome. **(7)** .... that we should expect anyone to give up eating meat forever, of course. Everyone should be **(8)** .... to make their own choices, whichever age they might be, as our two interviewees confirm.

Sara, 17, Madrid

It's fair to say that Spanish people have a love for meat that has existed for centuries. In Europe, we are second only to Luxembourg in terms of annual consumption of meat per person, and it's difficult to think of a traditional dish that doesn't include animal products, whether that means meat, fish, dairy or all three. This is traditionally not a country that has a great love for junk food or ready meals. Spain also has a huge number of critically acclaimed restaurants, the vast majority of which will predominantly serve meat, fish and dairy-based dishes. And our tapas are a celebration of how amazing animal produce can taste.

So why on earth, then, have I decided to abstain from these three core ingredients of our national cuisine and become a vegan? Well, it's not because I don't like the flavours that all these things can bring, that's for sure. My mum cooks the best meat-based dishes in the world and I desperately miss my favourite dessert – a rich and creamy rice dish called _arroz con leche_ (I even dreamed about it the other night).

The fact is, I have to follow my conscience. I feel a tremendous sense of compassion towards animals. I'm greatly committed to improving their welfare as a whole, as well as to the global issue of sustainability regarding food produce. And the number of vegans in Spain is growing rapidly. In fact, in 2020, Spain had the ninth-highest percentage of vegans in the world, which I'm absolutely delighted about, and organic food is becoming increasingly popular, too. Despite this, so many people still don't seem to grasp the fundamental part of being a vegan or vegetarian, which is this: we _do not_ eat meat – _ever_. Not even the tiny squares of meat in _croquetas_.

Dasha, 18, Moscow

Russian cuisine is dominated by meat. Apparently, about 20% of Russian people believe that not eating meat is really bad for your health. But, in my case, I knew from a very early age that I simply didn't like the way it tasted. Of course, I was too young to do much about it then, and it wasn't actually until I was fourteen that I stopped eating it entirely. From that point, everyone close to me kept warning that my diet would make me ill, and when I was sixteen, I was persuaded to start eating meat again. Despite it really affecting my health in a negative way, it was wonderful not to feel compelled to prove that vegetarianism was the way forward for me.

These days, if ever I go to a party or a family gathering, I usually have to spend about half an hour explaining why I'm a vegetarian and giving examples of what I eat. Not that people are rude about it; they are generally just confused about why I have made that choice. Vegetarianism was actually banned in Russia for many years in the 20th century, and this might be why quite a few older people here still strongly believe that vegetarians only exist because they have some sort of medical issue, rather than it being a matter of personal choice. 'One must eat meat to survive the winter' is an old saying that I've been hearing more frequently than ever before. But I'm always strong in my beliefs. This is my decision and I'm completely happy with it.

7 Match the highlighted words in the article to the meanings.

1 a party or a meeting when many people come together as a group ....
2 the basic and most important part of something ....
3 mostly or mainly ....
4 the amount used or eaten ....
5 physical and mental health and happiness ....

1 Rewrite the sentences using the passive. Choose whether it is appropriate to include or omit the agent.

1 You need to add sugar at the start of cooking tomatoes.

....

2 The head chef personally welcomes each guest to the restaurant.

....

3 Someone has put up posters advertising a new juice bar in town.

....

4 The government has created a new law that bans takeaway restaurants from using plastic containers.

....

5 My doctor has advised me to cut down on salt.

....

6 The longer you leave the dinner in the oven, the nicer it will taste.

....

2 Complete the sentences with the verbs in the box. You should use the verb form given in A–I.

add   burn   expect   install   invite
offer   prepare   serve   tell

0 On arrival, each of the guests ___will be offered___ a selection of snacks to stimulate their appetites. (A)

1 There's a scar on my left wrist from when I .... by an open flame while cooking. (B)

2 After the way you criticised the host's cooking, I'm not sure we're .... to dinner there again. (C)

3 The main course .... now, and the diners all seem really pleased with the way it looks. (D)

4 As the vegetables ...., the chef turned her attention to seasoning the meat. (E)

5 I can't help your mum put the washing up away because I .... where everything goes. (F)

6 This dish would have tasted amazing if a little more salt .... at the end of the cooking process. (G)

7 In Korea, if an older person offers you a drink, you .... to lift it to your mouth with both hands. (H)

8 After her new, state-of-the-art kitchen ...., the chef felt happier than ever. (I)

A future passive (with *will*)
B the *get* passive
C future passive (with *going to*)
D present continuous passive
E past continuous passive
F present perfect passive
G past perfect passive
H present simple passive
I past simple passive

3 The passive can be used in five of the eight underlined clauses. Choose which five and rewrite them in the passive. Put a cross by the clauses that cannot be changed.

🔍 What time do people have their dinner in different parts of Europe?

Generally speaking, [1] people eat dinner earlier in northern Europe. For example, in the Netherlands, where [2] they do not tend to serve hot meals during school lunch times, which are also quite short in duration, [3] people often sit down for dinner at some point between 5 pm and 7 pm. In some parts of northern England, [4] dinner takes place at around 1 pm, but this is simply an interesting aspect of local dialect as [5] they refer to their evening meal as 'tea'.

[6] People widely recognise Spain as a country where the evening meal rarely begins until around 9 pm. This is similarly true in India, where traditionally the family would only eat when the father or son returned from their agricultural work. [7] They haven't changed this tradition because city jobs now demand the same commitment in terms of working hours.

I remember once, [8] when I was staying in Lisbon, I went out with a friend and we didn't have a single bite to eat until long past midnight! That must surely be the latest I've ever eaten dinner.

1 ....
2 ....
3 ....
4 ....
5 ....

👁 **4** Correct the mistakes in the sentences or put a tick by any you think are correct.

1 I really fancied a couple of biscuits, but the packet had already been open and they had gone soft.

....

2 By 2025, I will have been being a vegan for ten years.

....

3 The recipe, according to my mum and my aunt, were handed down to them by my great-grandmother.

....

4 I absolutely love the smell of vegetables when they are cooked over an open fire.

....

5 Hector can't actually eat all the tomatoes he grows, so I think he's going to be sold some at the market.

....

6 The sink has been filled with water, so what are you waiting for? Get on with the washing up!

....

7 In most countries, tipping the waiter is common, but it isn't seeing as an obligation.

....

8 When she got to the restaurant, it was remembered by Anna that she had forgotten her credit card.

....

VOCABULARY
DESCRIBING FOOD: COLLOCATIONS

1 Match the two halves of the collocations.

1 free-		**a** sourced
2 freshly		**b** dried
3 gluten-		**c** range
4 home		**d** roasted
5 locally		**e** baked
6 pan-		**f** made
7 slow-		**g** fried
8 sun-		**h** free

1	3	5	7 ......
2	4	6	8 ......

2 Put a tick next to the correct sentences and a cross next to the incorrect sentences.

1 *Carretine* supermarkets are currently offering 12 **sun-dried** eggs for the price of 6. ......
2 It's so important that people try to eat **free-range** chicken and eggs as often as possible. ......
3 Mum has just got back from the market with some amazing **freshly baked** cheese. ......
4 **Slow-roasted** vegetables taste absolutely delicious. ......
5 Every Wednesday, my grandmother goes to the local fish market to get some **homemade** salmon. ......
6 Toni is a great chef. Her speciality of **pan-fried** chicken in garlic and herbs is absolutely amazing. ......
7 The hotel has a five-star restaurant that only serves **locally sourced** produce. ......
8 It can be difficult to find them, but I always make sure that I buy **gluten free** tomatoes. ......

3 Suggest alternative collocations for the incorrect sentences from Exercise 2.

Sentence ...... :

....

Sentence ...... :

....

Sentence ...... :

....

Sentence ...... :

....

FOOD AND DRINK: EXPRESSIONS

4 Match the phrases to form eating and drinking expressions.

1 Let's		**a** a sweet tooth.
2 It's on		**b** than your stomach!
3 Tuck		**c** easy on the spicy sauce!
4 Say		**d** in!
5 I could		**e** go halves.
6 Your eyes are bigger		**f** the house.
7 Go		**g** eat a horse!
8 I have		**h** when!

1	3	5	7 ......
2	4	6	8 ......

5 Correct the expressions in bold in the conversations.

1 **A:** I haven't got a lot of money at the moment, but I do want to take you somewhere nice for your birthday.
  B: Oh, you don't have to do that.
  A: I really would like to.
  B: Well, we can **go half** on dinner if you want?

  ....

2 **A:** What's your favourite part of a meal?
  B: I'm not sure I've got one. Yours?
  A: Oh, dessert, every time. I've got such a **sugar tooth**.

  ....

3 **A:** Here's your cappuccino, sir, and your loyalty card.
  B: Okay … what do I do with this?
  A: You get it stamped every time you come in and buy something. Once you've collected six stamps, you get a drink of your choice.
  B: What, a *free* drink?
  A: Yes, completely **on our house**. ....

4 **A:** Do you want some juice?
  B: Maybe. What is it?
  A: Watermelon – I've just made it myself.
  B: In that case, yes please.
  A: Okay, I'll pour you a glass … **say stop**!

  ....

5 **A:** I can't believe how many tapas you've ordered.
  B: Stop moaning, I'm hungry.
  A: There are eleven tapas on this table and only two of us.
  B: Stop moaning and **check in**!
  A: We'll never finish it all. Your eyes are far **wider than your stomach**! ....

6 **A:** You were gone for a long time. How far did you run?
  B: About 8 km.
  A: Wow. You must be thirsty.
  B: And hungry. Is dinner going to be ready soon? **I could eat a house**! ....

7 **A:** I'm making some Mexican *chilaquiles* for breakfast. Do you fancy some?
  B: Yeah, why not. But **go easy for** the chillies – you like them ridiculously hot. ....

6 Complete the sentences with the phrases from Exercises 4 and 5.

1 Okay, everyone, here are your main courses. Please, ... !
2 Dessert is my favourite part of a meal. I've got a really ....
3 Let's have dinner now. I'm so hungry, I .... !
4 The doctor has told me to .... the spicy food for a while. It clearly isn't good for me.
5 Will always orders too much food when we go out. His eyes are .... !
6 I'm not sure how much milk you like in your coffee, so .... !
7 When we went bowling for my birthday, the manager brought over some burgers – .... !
8 I don't expect you to pay for dinner for both of us. Shall we .... ?

LISTENING

1 Look at the pictures above. Which is closest to your cooking ability?

🔊 10 **2** Listen to the first part of an interview with a teenage chef, Kelis Maya. Which nouns do you hear in the final sentence? Listen twice if you need to.

3 Read the sentence. Which of the nouns from Exercise 2 can you add to form a grammatically correct sentence?

Kelis says that, after her win, she was most keen to discuss her _____ with journalists.

🔊 10 **4** Listen again to the first part of the interview. Which of your answers from Exercise 3 best completes the sentence?

5 Do you need to add any other words to your answer? Why? / Why not?

✓ 🔊 11 **6** Listen to rest of the interview. For questions 1–7, complete the sentences with a word or short phrase.

1 Once back at home, Kelis decided to develop her awareness of how _____ approach food preparation.

2 Kelis mentions that the _____ arranged by the show's producers was challenging.

3 Kelis confesses that she struggled with her _____ early on in the series.

4 Kelis mentions how cooking encourages people to seek _____ rather than focus on negative outcomes.

5 Kelis says that says that she likes to invest in some new _____ when she receives her prize money.

6 Kelis has concerns that her lack of skills in making _____ may slow down her training next year.

7 Kelis is keen to ensure that an understanding of _____ begins at an early age.

🔊 11 **7** Listen again and check your answers.

READING AND USE OF ENGLISH

1 Read the two lines of the online review below. What do you think the writer might say in their review of Café Arenal?

> Café Arenal – £ £ £ £ £
>
> ' … definitely worth the money … '

2 Read the review in Exercise 5 quickly, ignoring the gaps, and check your ideas.

3 What type of word do you need for each of the gaps 1–8 in Exercise 5?

> adjective   adverb   auxiliary verb
> preposition   verb

1 ....   3 ....   5 ....   7 ....
2 ....   4 ....   6 ....   8 ....

4 Which of the sentences could be used for gap (1) and why?

A I had read about it before we came.
B I had read up about it before we came.
C I had read on it before we came.
D I had read up on it before we came.
E I had read up it before we came.

5 Complete the review. For questions 1–8, think of the word which best fits each gap. Use only one word in each gap.

I was immediately conscious **(0)** _of_ its sheer quality from the moment I walked through the doors of Café Arenal, the first Michelin-starred restaurant I had ever been to. I had read up **(1)** .... it before we came, and the reviews were all saying the same thing – amazing food, very expensive. I'm certainly not rich, but it was my birthday, so why not **(2)** .... out on something special? We sat down and were given some warm, freshly **(3)** .... bread – the best I'd ever eaten, by far – and we knew we'd made the right choice.

With 20 courses on its tasting menu, I was initially wondering how I'd get **(4)** .... them all. I needn't have worried. Not only **(5)** .... each dish arrive beautifully presented, it was also the tastiest food I've ever eaten. Plus, I certainly didn't have to **(6)** .... out a loan to pay for it either – it cost far less than I'd expected. And when they found out it was my birthday, the waiters gave me three extra chocolate truffles at the end of the meal – **(7)** .... the house! What a perfect birthday! I only **(8)** .... I could go back every night.

6 Complete the table.

	Positive	Negative
Verb	decide	–
Noun		indecision
Adjective	decided	

7 Which word from the table in Exercise 6 is the correct answer to question (0) in the article in Exercise 9?

....

8 Which of the following suffixes can you correctly add to the noun *fear* to create an adjective?

1 -less   **3** -ity   **5** -ance
2 -ment   **4** -dom   **6** -ness

9 For questions 1–8, read the article. Use the word given in capitals at the end of some of the lines to form a word that fits in the gap in the same line.

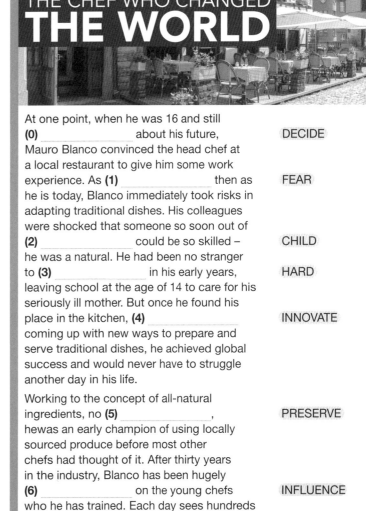

THE CHEF WHO CHANGED THE WORLD

At one point, when he was 16 and still **(0)** .... about his future, Mauro Blanco convinced the head chef at a local restaurant to give him some work experience. As **(1)** .... then as he is today, Blanco immediately took risks in adapting traditional dishes. His colleagues were shocked that someone so soon out of **(2)** .... could be so skilled – he was a natural. He had been no stranger to **(3)** .... in his early years, leaving school at the age of 14 to care for his seriously ill mother. But once he found his place in the kitchen, **(4)** .... coming up with new ways to prepare and serve traditional dishes, he achieved global success and would never have to struggle another day in his life.

Working to the concept of all-natural ingredients, no **(5)** .... , he was an early champion of using locally sourced produce before most other chefs had thought of it. After thirty years in the industry, Blanco has been hugely **(6)** .... on the young chefs who he has trained. Each day sees hundreds of people **(7)** .... trying to book a table at his restaurant, even though the hugely expensive meals there remain **(8)** .... to the average diner.

DECIDE

FEAR

CHILD

HARD

INNOVATE

PRESERVE

INFLUENCE

OPTIMIST

AFFORD

12 GREEN TRAVEL

1 Complete the words or phrases with the missing vowels.

1 c__rb__n n__ __tr__l
2 cl__n__ __p
3 __t__n__r__ry
4 b__ __nd f__ __r
5 __ff th__ b__ __t__n tr__ck
6 __ffs__t y__ __r c__rb__n f__ __tpr__nt
7 s__lf-c__t__r__ng
8 st__ __yc__t__ __n
9 s__st__ __n__b__l__ty
10 t__ __r__sm t__x

2 Replace the phrases in bold using a word or phrase from Exercise 1.

1 Flight number GA1634, **going to** Malaysia, is about to leave from gate number 6.
2 City breaks are okay, but I prefer somewhere **where few people go**, to be honest.
3 Although the buffets and restaurants in hotels can be great, I prefer a **holiday where I cook meals for myself.**
4 For the past couple of years, I've chosen to have a **holiday at home** rather than going abroad.
5 My dad spoils so many holidays by sticking to his **list of places he wants us to visit**; it makes everything so predictable.
6 It is only fair that governments charge a **tax for overseas visitors to stay in their country.** It helps local areas a lot.
7 All flights these days should include an additional option to **compensate for emissions by funding CO_2 savings elsewhere.**
8 On a walking holiday in the Alps, I couldn't believe that people didn't **remove rubbish and make things tidy in** the area – there was litter everywhere.
9 The aviation industry aims to be **not producing any carbon emissions or compensating for any they do produce** by 2050.
10 The biggest problem world tourism faces is **not causing environmental damage so it's able to continue for a long time**. Is this actually achievable?

3 Complete the sentences with the words and phrases from Exercises 1 and 2.

1 Alvaro looks happy … I would be as well, if I were _____ a month in the Maldives.
2 Right, who's got the _____? I've forgotten where we're supposed to be going next.
3 Nowadays, companies need to be _____ if they want to attract applicants from the next generation, who are highly conscientious when it comes to the environment.
4 We're not great fans of _____ breaks, mostly because neither of us can cook.
5 Most airline companies charge a fee that allows you to _____ on any journey.
6 Long-term environmental _____ will only be possible if governments make important changes today.
7 It's awful that people don't _____ their mess after they visit areas of natural beauty.
8 I can't afford to go abroad for my holiday this year. Looks like it's a _____ for me.
9 The campsite we stayed on was completely _____. It doesn't appear in any internet searches.
10 People complain about _____, but it's a completely fair way to make sure all visitors contribute to the local area.

4 Make notes to answer the following questions.

1 How can technology be used to recreate the experience of going on holiday?

2 What are the economic benefits and drawbacks of staycations?

3 In what way might contact with strangers affect a staycation?

4 What are the advantages of a staycation over a holiday abroad?

5 Read the four extracts in the article on the opposite page. Do you agree with the writers' ideas?

6 Answer the questions below.

Which writer

1 expresses a different view to B about the strength of the economic argument for staycations?
2 shares D's view about how successfully technology can re-create touristic experiences?
3 has a different opinion to the others about the way in which contact with new people affects a staycation?
4 has a different view to A about the extent to which staycations can help to improve holiday-makers' knowledge of history?

Should I **stay** or should I **go?**

A Belinda Miles

Thanks to the internet, arranging holidays is relatively straightforward. Not only are we exposed online to an infinite variety of beautiful and exciting-looking locations to visit worldwide, but the booking process is quick and user-friendly. However, while scanning the globe for potential destinations, we often fail to recognise what our own country can offer: an excellent, stress-free opportunity to explore our cities, towns and villages, and to learn about their rich and fascinating historical background. As long as you avoid getting overly familiar with local residents – who often regard tourists as an annoyance – you won't go far wrong. There is also an ethical case for holidaying in your own country: surely it is better to support local jobs and infrastructure by making sure that your hard-earned savings are invested in the domestic tourist sector, as opposed to internationally.

B Amrit Patel

What is there to recommend a staycation over a holiday abroad? Firstly, although chatting away with a foreign national in their own country can be great fun, it is ultimately more rewarding to interact in our own language with friendly faces from our home nation, widening our social network as we enjoy a well-deserved break. The main argument for staycations, however, centres on the financial advantages that internal tourism undoubtedly has for any country. In other aspects, the benefits of a staycation are less clear. For one thing, we are already familiar with our country's past and its landmarks; in that respect, there is more to be gained from venturing overseas. What's more, although many great museums worldwide offer virtual tours that can be viewed over the internet, these are little more than pale imitations of the real thing. The truth is that cultural exhibitions lose their effect if not seen in person.

C Doreen Strauss

Those who champion the staycation often claim we have a moral duty to go on holiday in our own country; doing so ensures that the money one might otherwise have spent abroad remains at home. Personally, I am yet to be convinced by this line of reasoning. There are, however, other more valid arguments for taking a staycation. For one thing, they have huge potential for life-enhancing interaction with others, whether bonding with family members at home or getting to know people in parts of your country that you may never have been to before. And these places often have a fascinating heritage to find out about when you are there. If you are still worried about missing out on the cultural experience of overseas travel, don't forget that world-famous galleries and museums in cities around the globe now offer highly credible online showcases of their collections. Why not pay them virtual visits while relaxing somewhere comfortable and familiar?

D Mario Rodriguez

Most people would say, and I would not necessarily disagree, that going on holiday abroad does much to open the mind and relax the soul – and it can often be done in a very affordable way. Nonetheless, it makes little sense to ignore what is on your own doorstep. Open your front door, jump on a train and take pleasure in the wonderful encounters that naturally occur with the people you meet along the way. Visit archaeological sites and other monuments. Investigate your roots – there is always so much to discover about what came before us. Stay at home and take advantage of the internet; it is such a wonderful tool for experiencing exhibitions or concerts that take place in other countries, generally with a high enough quality that you can imagine yourself experiencing them in person. Who needs a holiday abroad when you have all that?

---

7 Match the highlighted words in the article to the meanings.

1 support, defend or fight for a person, belief, right, or principle enthusiastically ....

2 improving the quality, amount or strength of something ....

3 features belonging to the culture of a particular society that were created in the past and still have historical importance ....

4 the process of thinking about something in order to make a decision ....

5 risk going somewhere or doing something that might be dangerous or unpleasant ....

GRAMMAR
PASSIVE GERUND AND INFINITIVE

1 **Match the sentence halves.**

1 On arriving at the hotel, they were furious
2 Guests who make too much noise at night risk
3 After all the problems with his flight, he insisted
4 Neve has bought factor 30 sun cream to avoid
5 If I were you, I'd probably consider
6 Without the mountain rescue team, he might
7 I'm going to be late – my taxi was supposed
8 Thousands of tourists are about

a to have arrived by now.
b getting burnt when she's in Greece.
c being shown around by a local guide.
d not to have been provided with someone to help with their luggage.
e to be informed their travel insurance is no longer valid.
f being asked to leave the hotel.
g never have been found.
h on being given a seat in first class.

| 1 .... | 3 .... | 5 .... | 7 .... |
| 2 .... | 4 .... | 6 .... | 8 .... |

2 **Correct the mistakes in the sentences or put a tick by any you think are correct.**

1 I never expected being upgraded to first class, so it was a wonderful surprise. ....
2 In Paris, we were lucky enough to make an amazing dinner by a world-famous chef. ....
3 All international travellers should be show how to become more carbon neutral. ....
4 Being allowed into the turtle rescue centre was a highlight of the trip for me. ....
5 Some people on flights demand being treated like royalty – it's so rude. ....
6 On arrival at the campsite, the guests were astonished to be informed that it was closed. ....
7 I'm really looking forward to be reunited when you come back home. ....
8 Have you seen my passport? I'm getting really worried about not to be able to find it. ....

3 **Complete the sentences with the verbs in brackets in the passive form.**

1 Pablo and Maria were such great hosts. I'm really going to miss .... to dinner every night. (take)
2 Given that we've paid for a tour guide, I'm expecting .... some amazing sights. (show)
3 Because of the air traffic controllers going on strike, all flights are likely .... (delayed)
4 I like flying, but can't stand constantly .... to put my seat up. I need to sleep on long journeys. (ask)
5 We both feel like .... today, so let's book ourselves into the health spa in the hotel. (spoil)
6 I always insist on .... (show) the emergency exits whenever I check into a hotel.
7 The family in the room next door really didn't appreciate .... to keep the noise down. (tell)
8 If there is a problem with the air conditioning, the guests will need .... immediately. (inform)

4 **Choose the correct options.**

1 *Being compared / Compared* with twenty years ago, global temperatures are increasing at a faster rate.
2 We were absolutely furious *being / to be* left completely alone in the jungle.
3 Rosa denied *having been / to have been* sent the email informing her of the increase in price.
4 My bag was too heavy *being / to be* allowed on the flight.
5 We all had a great time *being / to be* given a lesson in how to make a raft from logs and branches.
6 Saul was astonished *being / to be* ordered to pay a tourist tax of €150 on arrival.

PASSIVE STRUCTURES WITH TWO OBJECTS

5 **Write sentences so that there is one active sentence and two passive sentences.**

0 Active: My father bought me a surprise weekend away.
Passive 1: I was bought a surprise weekend away by my father.
Passive 2: A surprise weekend away was bought for me by my father.

1 Active: The air steward gave me my lunch tray.
Passive 1: I was given my lunch tray by the air steward.
Passive 2: ....

2 Active: My brother has promised me a trip to Paris.
Passive 1: ....

Passive 2: ....

3 Active: ....

Passive 1: ....

Passive 2: The visitors are currently being read the house rules by the host.

4 Active: Daniel's maths teacher gave him a prize for coming top in his exam.
Passive 1: ....

Passive 2: ....

5 Active: The restaurant will offer guests a choice of starter and main course.
Passive 1: ....

Passive 2: ....

6 Active: Our government has set strict new laws for
....
Passive 1: ....
international travellers by the government.
Passive 2: ....

VOCABULARY
FORMAL AND INFORMAL LANGUAGE

1 Match the formal words and phrases 1–10 to their informal equivalents A–J.

1 arrive		**a** get
2 become		**b** buy
3 construct		**c** show
4 depict		**d** let
5 investigate		**e** build
6 permit		**f** quit
7 purchase		**g** stop
8 prohibit		**h** manage to
9 succeed in		**i** get somewhere
10 resign from		**j** look into

1	3	5	7	9 ....
2	4	6	8	10 ....

2 Put the letters in the correct order to form the formal equivalent of the words or phrases 1–8.

0 give back	*truren*	*return*
1 take off	mevore	....
2 kid	lhcid	....
3 say	pexrses	....
4 wrong	cornierct	....
5 start	cmemcone	....
6 mate	niferd	....
7 dodgy	hdntiesos	....
8 bug	rivus	....

3 Complete the sentences with the most appropriate word from the formal/informal pairs.

> arrive/get here   child/kid   construct/build
> dodgy/dishonest   incorrect/wrong
> investigate/look into   purchase/buy
> resigned from/quit

1 It was such a stressful flight! We were stuck behind this annoying .... who wouldn't shut up for the whole journey.
2 We appreciate how eager our guests are to do some sightseeing, but regretfully the coach is not due to .... until later in the day.
3 Now that I've cut air travel out of my life, I think I could .... a pretty solid argument for everyone else in the world to do the same.
4 I'm so annoyed – I nearly missed my train because the screen was showing the .... departure time.
5 Frequent travellers will often choose to .... a new book before embarking on a train journey.
6 It's no wonder Pablo has just .... his job! It was unbelievable how much travelling around the country he had to do. Must have been a nightmare.
7 With the airline industry currently in a state of transformation, it would without doubt be a wise move to .... alternative ways of travelling overseas.
8 I couldn't believe such a short journey would cost so much. What a rip-off! I must have had a .... taxi driver.

4 Complete the sentences with the words in the box. You will have to change each word given to its more formal/informal equivalent.

> become   commence   ~~express~~   give back
> let   prohibit   shows   take off   virus

0 I wouldn't say I'm fluent, but I know how to ___say___ enough to get by.
1 Before passing through airport security, please .... your shoes to ensure that queues can be kept to a minimum.
2 I always .... anxious just before take-off, but once we're in the air, I'm fine.
3 In accordance with the law, Nebula Cruise Company does not .... animals on board apart from assistance dogs for people who are visually impaired.
4 Last year, I decided to .... a travel blog so that I could let everyone know what I was doing on my travels.
5 A new collection of photographs .... the ancient city of Petra in all of its inspiring beauty.
6 I reckon we could solve climate change easily if we could just .... people from flying. But of course, that would never happen.
7 My best friend came down with a nasty .... the day before we were due to set off, so she couldn't come on the trip.
8 Passengers are welcome to keep the souvenir raincoats but are obliged to .... the life jackets before they leave the ferry.

FORMAL AND INFORMAL WAYS OF EXPRESSING QUALITY

5 Choose the correct options.

1 We have had *numerous / loads of* high-quality applications for the position of tour guide, and we are delighted to offer you an interview.
2 I'm not that into camping – it always gets *rather / a bit* chilly and I find it tough getting to sleep at night.
3 It has been widely recognised for decades that air travel is responsible for *a large amount of / tons of* the pollution in the atmosphere.
4 Henrik got totally seasick when he was on the ferry – he'd gone green by the time he got off! He says he's *considerably / much* better now, though.
5 A short distance from the Shetland coast today, *large numbers of / loads of* Humpback Whales were spotted and filmed by delighted tourists.
6 It *doesn't matter much / matters little* where I sit – economy or first class. I just want to get there on time!
7 According to the latest scientific journals, because there are *so few / not many* polar bears in the wild, their future on the planet is in doubt.
8 I'm *pretty / rather* sure we don't need to pack a towel – all hotels have them these days, right?

WRITING A LETTER

» SEE *PREPARE TO WRITE* BOX, STUDENT'S BOOK PAGE 93

1 Make notes to answer the following questions.

1 What activities might an eco-friendly travel company offer?

2 Which of these activities would you enjoy? Why?

3 Which of these activities would you not enjoy? Why?

2 Read the task and answer the questions.

> You and a friend recently went on holiday with an eco-friendly travel company. During your stay, you visited two locations and took part in a range of environmentally friendly activities.
>
> Write a letter to the director of the company, Mr Eavis, saying what you did and didn't enjoy about your holiday and make suggestions for how you think it could be improved for visitors in the future.

1 Which of your ideas from Exercise 1 could you include in your letter?

2 How many sections/paragraphs would you include in your letter?

3 How would you start and finish your letter?

3 Read the opening of the sample answer. What is missing?

Dear Mr Eavis,

We were greatly impressed with the quality of the group walks in the countryside, most notably thanks to the warmth and impressive knowledge of David, our guide.

4 Look at the language used in the following examples. Which is the best way to start the letter?

Hey,

Me and my friend stayed with you recently and really enjoyed it. The beds were soooo comfy and we both got a lot out of the holiday. 5 stars!!

Dear Mr Eavis,

I am writing on behalf of me and my friend to say thank you for a wonderful holiday. The time we spent with your company was both comfortable and rewarding.

Dear Sir,

I am writing in order to extend my warmest gratitude and deepest thanks for the recent trip. You were kind enough to ensure that the stay was perfectly enjoyable and agreeable.

5 Read the next two paragraphs of the letter, ignoring the gaps, and answer the questions.

1 Does the writer address the question effectively?

2 What would they need to include in the paragraph after these?

3 Do they use a consistent style in both paragraphs?

We were greatly impressed with the quality of the group walks in the countryside, [1]_____ the warmth and impressive knowledge of David, our guide. [2]_____, on each of the four sites we stayed in, we were [3]_____ the chance to plant trees for the first time in our lives and were [4]_____ to find that all accommodation was entirely carbon neutral.

To improve the holiday further, how about this? The two accommodation sites are nowhere near each other and, while your company's aim to stop using petrol in cars and buses deserves praise, it took two hours on three trains to get from accommodation A to accommodation B. Oh, and another thing – tree-planting aside, you didn't put on anything else that would let us contribute to the sustainability of the local areas in which we stayed.

6 Complete the letter in Exercise 5 with the phrases in the box.

> Added to this   extremely pleased with
> hugely reassured   mostly thanks to

7 Read the second paragraph in Exercise 5 again and underline the sections of the text which are too informal.

8 Which of the underlined sections from Exercise 7 should these phrases replace?

1 I would suggest the following

2 there were no further opportunities to

3 located at an inconvenient distance from

4 eliminate its carbon footprint

5 Additionally

6 travel from one site to another

9 Create the third paragraph by putting the sentences in order. There is an extra sentence which you do not need to use.

A Although this would not be as carbon neutral as going by train, it could be compensated with a small carbon-offsetting charge when visitors first book their holidays.

B I would also recommend that you contact the chef to make sure that the meals are vegan, rather than vegetarian, as I mentioned before.

C In future, perhaps you could arrange for guests to be transported between sites on a minibus or coach.

D It would also be a positive move to offer additional activities that benefit the local environment, such as organising partnerships with local farms where guests could volunteer.

1 ....   **2** ....   **3** ....

10 Why does the extra sentence not fit well into this paragraph?

....

....

11 Read the task and use the questions to plan your reply.

> You recently read a magazine article about a journalist's first experience of an eco-holiday. The journalist wrote about how unenjoyable she found her holiday, particularly in terms of the available travel options, the high cost of staying in a luxury wooden eco-hut and the food. Write a letter to the editor of the magazine, Emily Livingstone, stating what you agreed with in the article and pointing out which complaints you felt were unfair. Suggest how the journalist could have a different experience in the future.

1 On an eco-holiday, what travel options would guests be encouraged to use?

2 Which travel options would they not be encouraged to use?

3 Can you think of any other accommodation options for an eco-holiday apart from a *luxury, wooden eco-hut*? Why might the journalist have been unhappy about the cost of where she stayed?

4 What food is likely/unlikely to be served on an environmentally-friendly eco-holiday?

12 Write your letter in 220–260 words.

13 LEARNING THE LINGO

VOCABULARY AND READING
COMMUNICATION: PHRASAL VERBS

1 Match the phrasal verbs to the definitions.

1 catch up on
2 burst out
3 get at
4 talk (somebody) out of
5 get by
6 brush up on
7 go on about
8 talk (somebody) into
9 come up to
10 take (something) in

a suddenly say or do something loudly
b improve your knowledge of something already learned but partly forgotten
c give or share the latest news on something
d approach somebody with a purpose in mind
e attempt to say or explain something in a way that is not clear
f have enough of something to live or deal with a situation, but with some difficulty
g continue talking about something in an annoying or boring way
h convince somebody not to do something
i understand the meaning of something
j convince somebody to do something

1	3	5	7	9
2	4	6	8	10

2 Complete the sentences with a phrasal verb from Exercise 1 in the correct form.

1 We had a great time in Munich, partly because I .... my German before we went and could speak to the locals.
2 Toni and I met for a coffee and managed to .... what's been going on in our lives recently.
3 I'd hate to work in a tourist information office, dealing with all those people who .... you all day long with the same questions.
4 What do you think your mum was .... when she asked me if I'd been helping you with your English homework?
5 Christine just tried to say 'hello' in Dutch to Ruud. He .... laughing and said her accent was terrible.
6 I'm going to France next month. My French isn't amazing but I'll be able to .... using what I learned at school.
7 Sofia .... about her trip to Sardinia for the past hour and I honestly can't listen to much more.
8 When I visited Chile, I often found it difficult .... what they were saying – they speak Spanish so quickly.
9 People often .... friends .... doing something that they themselves are too lazy to do.

3 Complete the sentences so that they are true for you.

1 At the moment, the thing I most need to catch up on is

2 The last time I burst out laughing was when

3 I don't know too much about ...., but I know enough to get by.
4 The last time someone talked me out of something was when

5 If I need to talk someone into something, I'll

6 The best way to take in new vocabulary so that you won't forget it is ....

4 What reasons might someone have for becoming multilingual?

5 Read the four reports on the opposite page quickly. Which argument appears in each report?

A Learning a new language can be extremely difficult.
B There is a huge sense of reward in learning a new language.
C Being multilingual enhances your career prospects.

6 Answer the questions.

Which person mentions

1 providing entertainment for their peers? ....
2 challenging someone else's expectations? ....
3 appreciating multilingualism at an early age? ....
4 deliberately ignoring previous learning? ....
5 overcoming concerns about their own abilities? ....
6 following a specific path to improvement? ....
7 doubting a spontaneous decision? ....
8 feeling restricted in particular environments? ....

7 Match the highlighted words in the article to the meanings.

1 very boring ....
2 cheerful and happy ....
3 rise to a very high level ....
4 continue doing something even though it is difficult ....
5 copy the way someone or something speaks, sounds or moves ....

RONNIE, 18

My family were always quite adventurous in their holiday destinations when I was little, and we would spend our summers in far-off places like Japan or Argentina. I'd always try to join in with the local kids' games, but would always end up disappointed because we couldn't speak the same language, and I could never quite understand exactly what they were getting at. I have a completely clear recollection of the exact moment I thought to myself, 'I wish I could talk to anyone in the world', and that dream has never left me. I'm now pretty fluent in five languages and have learned each one in the same way. Initially, I listen to national radio stations, hoping to notice common features of pronunciation. After that, I move onto films and use the subtitles to analyse the dialogue, before repeating it, which can take an entire afternoon. Only then will I start reading long texts or studying aspects of grammar. If I had the choice, I'd be focusing entirely on studying languages at college, even though my parents were never keen on me doing that. So I just have to do it when I get a spare hour or so.

SVETA, 25

I don't just see myself as someone who can chat to people or get by in seven languages – there is something more profound to it than that. For me, each language has its own strengths in expressing different aspects of my personality. Russian, for instance, is my mother tongue, and I use it when discussing intense matters or topics of intellectual weight; English is ideal for when I'm feeling light-hearted; French I find best suited to creativity. And, just as you wouldn't want to be in the same mood every day, I find myself desperate to escape if I spend too much time in a monolingual environment, as I feel so constricted when I'm surrounded by one single language. Interestingly, my primary school teacher warned me not to study languages at secondary school. She'd assumed I'd be hopeless at it because I was – and never have been – a high achiever, academically speaking. Now that I have a wonderful career as an interpreter, I'm grateful that I followed her advice as I learned these languages entirely by myself. If I'd studied in the conventional way at school, I expect I wouldn't have got anywhere close to where I am now.

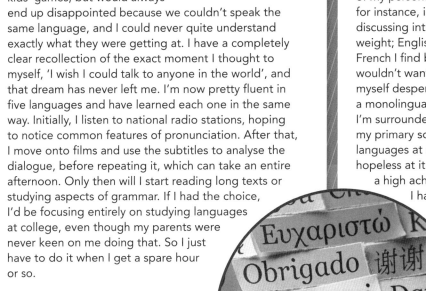

ROBERT, 24

If you'd met me in school, you would never have guessed that I'd end up with a working knowledge of four languages (additional to my own). I couldn't take anything in, I failed all my language exams and, by the time I reached the end of university, my only means of communication was still English. Even so, after graduation, I made a quick decision to move to Spain, ignoring anyone who tried to talk me out of it. Looking back, I still couldn't tell you what I was thinking at the time, and after six months there, I'd barely had a single conversation. Languages just weren't my thing, I concluded, and never would be. But life had become so tedious that I decided to stop making excuses and went for it. That first time I had a chat with someone was life changing, and I've never looked back since. It's not so much different from learning anything else, really. Getting started is the hardest part, but if you just soldier on, everything soon becomes less stressful. Once I'd stopped paying attention to the mistakes I was making, my worries disappeared, and my progress went through the roof.

SILVANA, 20

When I was growing up, I was obsessed with the sound patterns of the different accents that can be found in my country. I was always getting laughs by doing impressions of all the teachers. But it was much later, when I was 16 and at college, when I found myself in class with kids from other countries, that my fascination turned from imitating dialects to understanding languages. Now that I study at university overseas, I'm so proud to have become multilingual. Thanks to my earlier efforts, I can closely mimic the pronunciation and accents of a number of languages, and I regularly get mistaken for another nationality. When I'm learning a new language, it's almost as if my mind empties itself completely and I forget all the others I know. In fact, if you asked me a question in English at that point, I probably wouldn't be able to answer it. But that's the only way I can function. Even if I subconsciously make a connection between the grammar of one language and another, I force myself to ignore it.

GRAMMAR
CAUSATIVES

1 Correct the mistakes in bold.

1 My dad **had me to teach** him a few words in German before our holiday.

2 It's easy to **get someone help you** practise your speaking – there are lots of conversation apps available.

3 My sister is looking forward to **having done her nails** when she goes to the salon later.

4 I'm hoping to have my teachers **checked my university application** before I send it.

5 The tour guide was pretty good, but we had to **get her slowing down** when she was speaking.

6 When someone finds **to learn a language** difficult, you can't make them improve overnight.

7 My mum always used to **let us practised our English** on holiday, even though we were terrible at it.

2 Put the words in order to make sentences.

1 yesterday / bag / had / Mia / her / stolen

2 an hour / can't / you / me / wait / believe / I / made / for

3 my homework / by / going / to / I'm / get / checked / my sister

4 the teacher / to / his grade / improve / He's / to / trying / get

3 Rewrite each sentence, using *have* or *get*.

1 Marco asked Simon to check his homework – and he did.

2 I'm going to take my bike back to the shop so they can repair it.

3 I needed to translate a document into English, so I asked my cousin in London to help.

4 It's about time we invited your grandmother to visit.

5 Your laptop is broken. You should ask your parents to buy you a new one.

6 Miriam never walks to school – she always makes sure her mother drives her.

4 Correct the mistakes in the sentences or put a tick by any you think are correct.

1 She couldn't remember whether or not she had her coursebook put in her bag.

2 We should set different lunch times to avoid having students to queue at the same time.

3 We need to have the students register for the exam at least a month in advance.

4 After hours of trying, they finally succeeded in getting the cooker work.

5 For questions 1–6, complete the second sentence so that it has a similar meaning to the first sentence, using the word given. Do not change the word given. You must use between three and six words, including the word given.

1 Please ask someone to send the documents directly to me.
BE
Could you please arrange for
_____ directly to me?

2 We really should have employed an experienced professional to teach our English classes.
TAUGHT
We really should _____ by an experienced professional.

3 I regret asking for my hair to be cut in this ridiculous style.
NEVER
I should _____ in this ridiculous style.

4 James's car wasn't repaired because he forgot to take it to the garage.
SUPPOSED
James was _____ at the garage, but he forgot.

5 He will only eat meals that his favourite chef cooks.
COOKED
He insists on _____ by his favourite chef.

6 After forgetting his homework, his teachers kept him back after class.
MADE
After forgetting his homework, _____ after class by his teachers.

VOCABULARY
ADVERBS

1 Complete the crossword, using the definitions to help you.

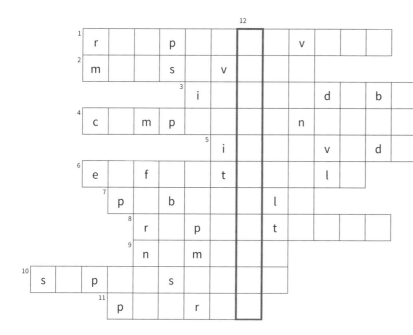

1 refers to things that have been mentioned, in the same order as they were mentioned
2 extremely or very much
3 very difficult to believe
4 completely; in a very clear and convincing manner
5 separately; on their own
6 in a way that is successful and achieves what you want
7 in a way that everyone might know about it
8 many times; again and again
9 in a specific way that gives more detail
10 according to what is said, claimed or believed by some
11 in an inferior or unacceptable way

2 Which is the correct definition for number 12 in Exercise 1?

A according to an accepted understanding of rules or facts
B using technology to do something
C in a way that shows the characteristics of someone/something

3 Choose the correct options.

1 Hungarian has a *namely / massively* complex grammar system.
2 Although you did not *technically / publicly* use it to cheat in the exam, you still should have turned your phone off before you entered the room.
3 To the eyes of many Europeans, East Asian languages are *incredibly / effectively* beautiful in written form.
4 In class, we tend to practise pronunciation first as a group before the teacher nominates students to speak *individually / respectively*.
5 Over the past year, this college has *supposedly / repeatedly* stressed its commitment to the development of strategies for language learning.
6 My dad only had a few lessons in English, French and Portuguese, but he's fluent in all three. He is *respectively / effectively* a self-taught multilinguist.

4 The words in bold are incorrect. Write the correct alternative from Exercise 1.

1 We haven't **respectively** covered every page of the course book, but we've learned more than enough to improve. ....
2 My two sisters, Lulu and Nila, are at university studying literature and maths **namely**. ....
3 When a vocabulary notebook is **publicly** organised, there is little chance that it will help the learner.
....
4 According to the website, my college **comprehensively** offers after-school language classes, but I don't think they exist. ....

5 Complete the sentences with the correct adverbs. Which of the statements do you agree with?

1 To learn a language e___f___t_____y, it's vital to spend time with native speakers.
2 Whilst it's challenging to read a novel in another language, it's also i___c___d_____y rewarding.
3 It's t___h n_____ly much more difficult to master grammar than it is to have a spoken conversation.
4 If you are unable to pronounce each sound within a word i___v___d_____y, you will never be confident in your pronunciation.
5 Being able to say that you can use a language c___p___h___s_____y requires you to master all of the skills – reading, listening, speaking and writing.

LISTENING

1 Which of the following are examples of non-verbal communication'?

facial expressions

body language

hand gestures

eye contact

distance from other person/people

2 Which of the following statements do you agree with? Why? / Why not?

1 Non-verbal communication adds emotion to what you are saying.

2 It can be confusing to other people.

3 It helps support what you are saying.

4 It is the main way that people communicate with each other.

 3 You will hear an interview with two researchers, Daniel Shu and Mia Cecchi, who are talking about non-verbal communication. Listen to the first part of the interview and make notes on what Daniel says regarding the questions in Exercise 2.

 4 Look at the question below. Listen again to the first part of the interview and choose the correct answer.

1 What point does Daniel make about non-verbal communication?

A It is vital when people intend to add clarity to what they are saying.

B It is often used in a way that can be confusing to other people.

C It is effective in assisting the process of spoken interaction.

D It is correctly believed to be the main way people express information.

5 Read the transcript of what Daniel said. **Highlight** where you find the correct answer.

Well, the first thing is to address the common misunderstanding that being a good communicator is almost nothing to do with the words you choose, but is actually about what you're doing when you say them. In our view, successful non-verbal communication works as a supportive companion to the language used, rather than as a dominant partner. For example, if I introduced myself in the conventional way – 'hello, I'm Daniel' – but had my back turned to you, you'd know what I was getting at, but it would still come across as completely strange. Basically, you can suggest something without using words, but language is there to verbalise ideas and make your meaning clear.

6 In a different colour, **highlight** the words or phrases that might attract you away from the correct answer.

 7 Listen to the rest of the interview. For questions 2–6, choose the answer (A, B, C or D) which fits best according to what you hear.

2 According to Daniel, what is their main aim in creating the website?

A to provide guidance for people in their interactions with others

B to ensure that any visitor to the site is entertained

C to maximise their chances of enjoying a high income

D to show off their extensive knowledge of relevant academic studies

3 Daniel mentions his difficulties when speaking Russian to explain that

A he had spent insufficient time studying the language.

B he wishes he had been from a different country.

C he felt embarrassed about his friendly personality.

D he had incorrect expectations of cultural similarities.

4 How does Mia suggest that an interviewee can benefit from controlling their body language?

A It helps them to create a connection with the interviewer.

B It allows them to appear more dominant.

C It forces them to consider the feelings of others.

D It encourages them to express themselves more creatively.

5 Mia says that when someone touches their nose, it

A proves whether or not they are telling the truth.

B performs a function that depends on context.

C confirms which country they come from.

D indicates to the listener that they trust them.

6 When discussing learning another language, Mia and Daniel agree that

A educational material should focus more on intercultural understanding.

B languages are most effectively taught by native speakers.

C people find it easier to develop their communication skills in local settings.

D lessons delivered in classrooms are unlikely to encourage progress.

READING AND USE OF ENGLISH

1 Read the article in Exercise 5 quickly, ignoring the gaps. What is the writer's main point?

A People learn languages more easily at school.
B People learn languages when they have time to study.
C People learn languages at different rates from each other.

2 Look at the first paragraph in Exercise 5. Which of gaps 1–3 should you use the words below in?

A an adverb ....
B an adjective ....
C a noun ....

3 For questions 1–3, only one of the following answers is correct. Which one?

A bearable
B comprehensible
C requirements

4 For questions 1–8, read the article. Use the word given in capitals at the end of some of the lines to form a word that fits in the gap in the same line.

Learning foreign languages

For many students, getting from A to B in their language skills is often a **(0)** _painfully_ slow process, full of frustration and increasingly **(1)** _____. Others seem to enter each class having **(2)** _____ covered every aspect of the lesson before it even begins. Their teachers confidently predict these talented individuals will fulfil all given academic **(3)** _____ that will enable them to study languages at university.

So, what can the less confident language student do? The internet is full of adverts for language courses which will **(4)** _____ turn you into a gifted linguist overnight. They talk of students who have battled against **(5)** _____ and ended up with the highest grades, all by following the simple **(6)** _____ that they provide. It may work for some people, but, in all **(7)** _____, these claims will be false. The fact is, there are no shortcuts to effective language learning. But one thing is certain – finding it difficult does not necessarily mean you are **(8)** _____ of learning. Being conscientious is key.

PAIN

BEAR
COMPREHEND

REQUIRE

SUPPOSE

ADVERSE

GUIDE

LIKELY

CAPABLE

5 Which of the following options means the same as *eBooks are just as expensive now …* ?

A ebooks are down in price …
B ebooks came down in price …
C ebooks have not come down in price …
....

6 Underline the options that mean the same as *… as they were 10 years ago*?

through / over / since / in the last 10 years

7 Complete the second sentence so that it has a similar meaning to the first sentence, using the word given.

1 Surprisingly, ebooks are just as expensive now as they were 10 years ago.
DOWN
Surprisingly, ebooks have _____ the last 10 years.

8 For questions 2–6, complete the second sentence so that it has a similar meaning to the first sentence, using the word given. Do not change the word given. You must use between three and six words, including the word given.

2 It was a mistake to start writing the essay without planning it carefully first.
SHOULD
You _____ essay without planning it carefully first.

3 You don't often find prices as low as this in supermarkets.
SUCH
Rarely _____ in supermarkets.

4 My first encounter with Italian came from my grandmother.
INTRODUCED
It _____ to Italian.

5 I regret not considering my choice of study partner more carefully.
THROUGH
If _____ my choice of study partner more carefully.

6 If you come over before six, I might still be eating dinner.
FINISHED
If you come over after six, I _____ then.

VOCABULARY AND READING
SOCIAL MEDIA MARKETING

1 Find the words related to social media and complete the gaps.

gysosponsoropeisboostyiengagewithtapdinifanbaseemfollowerolimarketcyor

soliaproductplacementargingemulatexterantargetialidesignergoodsobeanitan

1 b................	**5** m................	**9** d............ g............
2 e................	**6** t................	**10** p............ p............
3 s................	**7** f................	
4 f................	**8** e............ w............	

2 Match the definitions to the words and phrases from Exercise 1.

1 direct advertising or a product at someone ....

2 improve or increase something ....

3 products made by a famous or fashionable designer
....

4 pay for someone to do something or for something to happen
....

5 the fans of a singer, group, influencer, etc.; considered as a group ....

6 a way of advertising a product by supplying it for use in films or television programmes ....

7 a person who has a great interest in someone or something
....

8 copy something achieved by someone else and try to do it as well as they have ....

9 become involved with someone or something ....

10 make goods available to buyers in a planned way that encourages people to buy more of them, e.g. by advertising
....

3 Complete the article with words or phrases from Exercise 1.

4 You are going to read an extract from an article about fake news on the opposite page. Six paragraphs have been removed from the extract. Choose from the paragraphs A–G the one which fits each gap (1–6). There is one extra paragraph which you do not need to use.

5 Match the highlighted words in the article to the meanings.

1 having to do something because you are forced to or feel it is necessary ....

2 something that causes concern or anxiety
....

3 in a way that is completely enthusiastic and without any doubt ....

4 if not; in another way ....

5 only; just ....

Make way for the Influencers

Sales of celebrity magazine *Watch!* were ¹................ after the appearance of Taylor Swift as this month's cover star resulted in her loyal ²................ buying thousands of copies. This has come as a relief to the magazine owners, who have been complaining about the problems print journalism faces when it attempts to ³................ and sell its products. 'While we do our best to ⁴................ today's trends, it is never easy to compete with online sites, which are able to easily ⁵................ the readers that we are so keen to attract.'

This much is certainly true. Although readers often express annoyance with constantly seeing ads containing ⁶................ on their screens, it doesn't seem to have sent them hurrying back to print magazines. Indeed, despite the popularity of singers like Taylor Swift, social media influencers have, in many cases, overtaken musicians as the public figures that young people want to ⁷................ . They can boast of having millions of ⁸................ who turn to them for advice on cosmetics, for example, or exclusive ⁹................ . Whereas in the past, advertisers would pay healthy sums of money to get their products in popular magazines, today they ¹⁰................ these new stars who have such a massive effect on consumer lifestyles. With this type of competition for young people's attention, it is no wonder the likes of *Watch!* magazine are experiencing tough times.

No News is Good News

Today, the likelihood of young people reading (and trusting) fake news is higher than ever. Last year, when 17-year-old Rabia was given a project for her media studies course instructing her to engage with online sources of information and evaluate whether are they are trustworthy, she initially thought little of it. She was confident in her ability to distinguish fake news from real news. To get her started, her teacher gave her a set of worksheets to use as a basis for her research.

1

The results showed how easily the 'digital natives' of Generation Z are able to switch between, and engage fully with, several social media accounts all at once. But there was also a hugely troubling conclusion. After assessing almost 8,000 students, all around Rabia's age or slightly older, the researchers found that the majority of them were entirely incapable of objectively assessing what they saw and read.

2

Given how personally Rabia took this claim, she felt compelled to investigate further and went hunting for different sources that she hoped would confirm her first ideas. Pleasingly for her, she was able to find the information she needed to reassure herself that she and her friends were not what had been suggested, but were actually quite analytical and sophisticated internet users.

3

Interestingly enough, during her searches, Rabia read something about a concept that was highly relevant to this: *confirmation bias*. This is when people search for, interpret and remember information purely to support and authenticate their existing beliefs. It was at this moment that Rabia really started to question herself and her research findings. What she had been doing, clearly, was refusing to accept the result of a published academic study because she objected to the idea that her friendship group could all be easily targeted and tricked by lies dressed up as authentic news.

4

She decided to find out, and asked three of her most trusted friends to read the Stanford study and give their reactions to it. The first became doubtful of the research, in the same way that Rabia herself had been initially. The other two, however, agreed wholeheartedly with the conclusions, confessing that they would believe most of what they read as long as it was presented in a familiar format, and would consider all information within it to be reliable.

5

Our educators and institutions spend a great deal of time and energy on boosting critical thinking as an essential skill in the 21st century. We are taught to analyse and assess the facts being presented. But this no longer seems sufficient, as we can't be sure of whether the 'facts' are actually facts at all. What is more, in the online world, 'native advertisements' – paid advertising which is designed to emulate the appearance of genuine editorial content – make things even more difficult. So, when ads no longer even look like ads, but work more like product placement, the less possible it becomes to blame anyone for being confused.

6

In many cases, it is impossible to say for certain. But, without the ability to differentiate between real and fake news, young people face more dangers online than we could ever have anticipated. They must be equipped with the skills to tell fact from fiction. As must we all.

A This generally came from a failure to question whether the data being used to support an opinion piece was reliable. Apparently, many even found it impossible to make a distinction between news articles and adverts. 'That's ridiculous, I'm not like that', she thought. 'No one my age is.'

B The main problem in this first situation is that it leads to more confusion, as the person reading the article, or seeing the advert start to forget what is real and what is fake. And this, of course, is the main aim for anyone posting fake news.

C Rabia was shocked. While she had not expected them all to think in exactly the same way as her, she certainly did not expect the opposite. Clearly, young people were vulnerable to believing fake news. She began to consider who should be taking responsibility for teaching them otherwise.

D And this is the point. It is no wonder that people like Rabia are feeling the pressure of constantly having to consider not just what is being said, but also who is saying it, and why. What do the writers of whatever she happens to be reading hope to gain?

E The more she thought about it, though, the more she realised that they very rarely discussed the current affairs with each other. They were too concerned that everyone else might laugh at them for being so poorly informed. So how could she have truly known what her peers believed?

F One included part of a report from Stanford University titled 'Evaluating Information'. This gave details about a study of how well primary school, secondary school and college students were able to evaluate online sources of information. While the evidence-based findings were clear, it was certainly depressing to read them.

G Of course, when you do your own research, and look online for long enough, eventually you will pretty much always find something to confirm your view. It might take you a while, but somewhere on the internet, there will be a page to prove your point.

GRAMMAR
REPORTED SPEECH

1 **Rewrite these direct speech statements and questions in reported speech.**

1 'I'll send you a link to an amazing news website.'
Dominic told me ....

2 'I haven't read the article, but I do plan to when I get home this evening.'
Christina said ....

3 'I'm so pleased; I've completely cleaned up my friends list.'
Stefan said ....

4 'I've been planning to do a media course since last year.'
Victoria said ....

5 'I'm not sure when the homework is due, but I'll ask our teacher.'
Xavier said ....

6 'Which online news providers do you subscribe to?'
Marianna asked me ....

7 'I might not be able to visit you next week.'
Simon told me that ....

8 'It's OK to be worried about your exams, but I'm sure they will be fine.'
Lara told me ....

9 'The internet is a useful resource, but you shouldn't trust everything you read online.'
My teacher said ....

10 'I hadn't realised that my maths homework would be so difficult until I started it.'
Luisa told me ....

2 **Choose the correct options.**

1 Scientists have *advised / recommended* people to spend no more than 90 minutes online each day.
2 As I left for college, my mother *explained / reminded* me to be home by 5 pm for my grandfather's birthday party.
3 Jonas *admitted / promised* using his sister's password to log into her social media accounts.
4 The university course advisor *encouraged / suggested* selecting media studies as my first choice.
5 We are delighted to have *persuaded / admitted* popular influencer LitlClix to endorse our latest range of products.
6 At Novelomedia, we *promise / insist on* providing readers with the most reliable news on the planet.
7 The research *concluded / decided* that interaction patterns on social media are more predictable than first imagined.
8 My teacher *reassured / recommended* me that she would do everything she could to help me pass my exams.

3 **Use impersonal reporting structures to avoid saying who the reporter is.**

0 Apparently, people's brains are totally different from 100 years ago, thanks to technology. (say)
It is said that people's brains are totally different from 100 years ago, thanks to technology.
1 Last week, a journalist published an article saying that 50% of the news we read today is fake. (report)
....
2 Yesterday, the government told everyone that every home will have fibre optic broadband by 2024. (announce)
....
3 Most people are pretty sure that all aspects of life will be run online by 2050. (assume)
....
4 There are thousands of people who think that the internet should never have been invented. (believe)
....

4 **Rewrite the sentences using the reporting verbs from the box.**

| deny | ~~invite~~ | offer | suggest | warn |

0 Dusan: 'Paola, why don't you come over and watch a movie with me later today?'
Dusan invited Paolo to come over and watch a movie with him later that day.
1 Sophie: 'If I were you, I'd try cutting down on the amount of time you spend on social media.'
....
2 Antonio: 'Danique, don't open that file! It's got a virus!'
....
3 Gabriela: 'Dad, I wasn't at home when the TV got smashed.'
....
4 My mum: 'I'll help you with your homework as long as you tidy your bedroom first.'
....

5 **Correct the mistakes in the sentences or put a tick by any you think are correct.**

1 The headteacher called us into his office and said us that we were going to be disciplined. ....
2 Yesterday, she said she accepts my invitation to work as study partners on the project. ....
3 Eric arrived home after months away and, before he could tell anything, his mother burst into tears. ....
4 Maria promised she would always look out for me, whatever happens. ....

VOCABULARY
NEGATIVE PREFIXES AND SUFFIXES -FUL and -LESS

1 Choose the correct negative prefix to change the words into nouns, adjectives or adverbs.

	Nouns		Prefixes to use
1 able	**1** _inability_		
2 mature	**2**		de-
3 comfortable	**3**		dis-
4 literate	**4**		il-
	Verbs		im-
5 obedience	**5**		in-
6 done	**6**		ir-
7 activated	**7**		un-
8 belief	**8**		
	Adjectives		
9 health	**9**		
10 efficiently	**10**		
11 qualification	**11**		
12 precision	**12**		
	Adverbs		
13 rationality	**13**		
14 patience	**14**		
15 cooperate	**15**		
16 responsibility	**16**		

2 Complete the words with the correct negative prefix.

1 A lot of tech companies are using people's personal data ....responsibly, which is leading to a lack of trust.

2 I often experience a certain amount of ......comfort when reading some friends' social media posts.

3 It's ......healthy to spend too much time on social media as it can lead to feelings of stress and anxiety.

4 I needed a break from social media, so I decided to ......activate my Instagram account.

5 Some influencers ......obey the rules and don't make it clear enough when they are advertising a product on behalf of a company.

6 One problem with having constant access to the internet and social media is that it leads to an ......ability to switch off at the end of the day.

3 Complete the sentences using the answers from Exercise 1.

1 A very serious concern around fake news and information is that you sometimes see .... people, rather than genuine doctors, giving medical advice.

2 Seeing so many perfect images on Instagram can make young people behave ....; they place too much importance on things which don't deserve it.

3 There are laws in place that stop brands from using .... information in their adverts.

4 It's becoming easier and easier to make people .... the truth, even when it is supported by research or factual data.

5 In many western countries, children learn coding and IT skills from the age of 5 or 6, so computer .... is never going to be a problem.

6 The problems around fake news often arise because the 'Tech Giants' are acting .... with the authorities – they absolutely need to work together better.

4 Complete the sentences. Change the words in brackets by adding the correct prefix/suffix from the box below.

> anti-   -ful (x2)   -less (x3)   mis-   non-   un-

1 Thousands of people gathered together in the capital yesterday in a huge .... protest. (government)

2 The newspaper editor was found guilty of professional .... and was immediately fired. (conduct)

3 She made a peaceful, ... protest against the destruction of the forest. (violent)

4 The prime minister made an unplanned, ... remark about teenagers that upset thousands of young people. (thought)

5 We were left completely .... when our car broke down in the mountains. (help)

6 It's .... to speculate on whether the story is true or not – we need to do more research first. (use)

7 Adverts are often completely .... – they tell obvious lies in order to sell their products. (truth)

8 I've been trying to put together this new desk, but the instructions are so badly written and .... (help)

5 For questions 1–8, read the text below. Use the word given in capitals at the end of some of the lines to form a word that fits in the gap in the same line. The first word is given as an example.

QUITTING SOCIAL MEDIA

Cybersecurity expert Jeff Woodcock has no **(0)** _complaints_ about his job. 'Even after 20 years in this field, I still get plenty of **(1)** .... from solving IT problems,' he says. 'It's different with social media.'   COMPLAIN / FULFIL

A year ago, Jeff had become so uncomfortable about the impact social media had on his life that he **(2)** .... all his accounts. 'I'd been a prolific user for years,' he says. 'So when I told friends and colleagues I was quitting everything, their reaction was one of utter **(3)** ....'   ACTIVE / BELIEVE

'I'd reached a point where I was **(4)** .... looking at my phone,' explains Jeff. 'I'm not against social media in principle, though many of the comments people post can hardly be called **(5)** .... , and some online behaviour is clearly **(6)** .... It's more that I was spending hours a day **(7)** .... scrolling through my accounts. And I was always checking the notifications that were popping up, even though I knew it was **(8)** .... to do so. I've got much more time for the things that really matter now.'   EVER / THINK / ACCEPT / END / RATIONAL

>> SEE *PREPARE TO WRITE* BOX, STUDENT'S BOOK PAGE 109

1 Make notes to answer the following questions.

1 How much time do you spend on social media while in school or college?

2 What do you most frequently use social media for while in school or college?

3 Should social media be banned during school or college hours? Why? / Why not?

2 Read the task. Who is the report for? What style should it be written in?

> You and your year group have completed a week-long experiment in which you were instructed to avoid all social media access while in college. Your headteacher has asked you to write a report on your findings of the experiment. In your report, you should evaluate the positives and negatives of the experiment and make recommendations for future social media use in college. Write your **report** in 220–260 words.

3 Look at the plan written by a student. Which of the sections should *not* be included?

Section 1: Overview of social media – what it is and how it is used in society

Section 2: Outline of the experiment – who participated, time/duration

Section 3: Positives – students more focused in class, increased participation in sports during break times, more interaction during self-study periods, feeling of being more productive

Section 4: Negatives – unable to speak to friends/peers in other parts of the building, feeling of boredom and being controlled by teachers, unhappier with the situation by the end of the week

Section 5: Recommendations for future – limited use of 'no social media' policy

4 Read the report quickly, ignoring the gaps. Choose the best heading for each section (A–D).

1 Was it all worth it?
2 Outline of the experiment
3 Suggestions for the future
4 Focusing on the future – *our* future
5 Who told us to do the experiment
6 Drawbacks of the experiment
7 Successes of the experiment
8 What we did in the experiment

A _____

Dear Mr Smith,

In response to concerns raised by teachers that students were becoming less focused on their studies, the school conducted an experiment in which students from year 12 were instructed to avoid all use of social media during school hours for one week.

B _____

[1] _____, students were comfortable without social media access, and most reported higher levels of concentration in classes. There was also a visible increase in sports participation, not only during school hours, but also [2] _____, when the students had their smart phones back. [3] _____, there had been a general impression that self-study periods were purely for enjoying social media. [4] _____, however, the atmosphere in those periods was more productive and focused on work.

C _____

On the first day, students were happy to conduct all conversations face-to-face. However, [5] _____, the majority of them felt frustrated at not being able to communicate with friends through their favourite apps, particularly during break times. Additionally, a significant number also complained of boredom during break times, a feeling which [6] _____ turned into annoyance with teaching staff at being denied their smart phones, and most students began to feel more negatively about the experiment.

D _____

While there were clearly some successes that came out of the experiment, most students had become tired of it by the middle of the week. I would suggest a limited use of the 'no social media' policy, either for one full day or two half-days per week.

Yours sincerely,

Vladimir

5 Is there anything in the report that should not have been included?

_____

6 Complete the gaps 1–6 in the report with the correct word or phrase from the box. There are two that you do not need to use.

> afterwards   ahead of   beforehand   eventually
> initially   next   on a later day during the week
> subsequently

7 Choose the correct options. More than one option may be correct.

1 There were a number of technical problems, but _in the end / at a later date / afterwards_, most course participants went home happy.
2 Last month's training day was a resounding success and there has _subsequently / at a later date / afterwards_ been a huge increase in interest in next month's session.
3 The organisers were concerned that the _initial / subsequent / latter_ response to the survey had been poor, so they decided to offer prizes for participation.
4 While the grades will be announced today, the certificates are scheduled to be handed out _at a later date / initially / afterwards_.
5 Attendees were fully engaged during the morning sessions, but their attention decreased in the _later / latter / afterwards_ part of the day.
6 Some students became upset during one of the talks, so in future I recommend that you provide _prior / previous / earlier_ warning of all content.
7 We had allocated 90 minutes for the first three lectures. _Afterwards / Subsequently / Latter_, we opened the debate to questions from the audience.
8 Both students and teachers expressed a great deal of excitement _ahead of / beforehand / subsequent_ their results coming in.

8 Complete the sentences using the sequence linkers in the box.

> afterwards   ahead of   at a later date   beforehand
> immediately   initially   latter   prior

1 There isn't enough time to complete the report now, so we will have to return to it _____ that we can all agree on.
2 During the experiment, most students were dismissive of its potential benefits. _____, however, they agreed it had been a success.
3 After much discussion about whether to limit social media use in class or to ban mobile phones completely, the _____ suggestion was rejected.
4 Many students were _____ reluctant to participate in the experiment, but changed their minds after some persuasion.
5 Permission slips will be sent to parents for their signatures _____ the school trip.
6 Attendees expressed satisfaction with the fact that, _____, they had been asked about their preferences for lunch, and as a result greatly enjoyed the meals on offer.
7 The new app was hugely popular, even with participants who had little or no _____ experience of this approach to social media.
8 As soon as the database hack was discovered, all participants were _____ contacted and advised to change their passwords as soon as possible.

✅ **9** Read the task and write your report.

> You and your year group have been invited to spend two weeks testing a new app which claims to help teenagers with their language learning. Your headteacher has asked you to write a report on your findings. In your report, you should summarise the positives and the negatives of the app, and make recommendations for its use in college.
> Write your **report** in 220–260 words.

VOCABULARY AND READING
WILDLIFE CONSERVATION

1 Complete the words with the missing vowels.

1 h __ b __ t __ t l __ ss
2 p __ __ ch __ ng
3 d __ cl __ n __ ng p __ p __ l __ t __ __ n
4 w __ ld __ rn __ ss
5 w __ __ dl __ nd
6 on the v __ rg __ of __ xt __ nct __ __ n

2 Match the definitions to the words or phrases from Exercise 1.

1 land on which many trees grow _____
2 the disappearance of natural environments that are home to particular plants and animals _____
3 when the members of a species are becoming fewer in number _____
4 an area of land which is neglected or difficult to live and farm on as a result of its extremely cold or hot weather or bad earth _____
5 in clear and immediate danger of not existing any more _____
6 catching and killing animals without permission on someone else's land _____

3 Complete the sentences with the words or phrases from Exercise 1.

1 Some very rare and special plants grow in the _____ close to my grandmother's cottage.
2 Many countries have a _____, as people tend not to have as many children as they used to.
3 The northern part of my country is cold and rocky _____ where very little grows.
4 _____ is a huge threat to millions of species, as the world's forests, lakes and other natural environments continue to disappear.
5 I believe that there should be much longer sentences for _____; it's terrible how people get away with killing animals illegally.
6 The Amur leopard is on the _____, and there may be none left in the wild by the end of this year.

4 Look at the pictures below. Which of the animals do you think the conservation status *vulnerable* is most likely to refer to?

Brazilian tapir   **jaguar**   **yacare caiman**

Extinct   Threatened   Least Concern

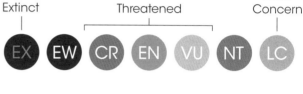

EX   EW   CR   EN   VU   NT   LC

5 Read the first paragraph of the article on the opposite page, ignoring the gaps. What do you learn about the conservation status of the animals in Exercise 4?

6 For questions 1–8, read the first paragraph of the article and think of the word which best fits each gap. Use only one word in each gap.

7 Read the rest of the article and choose the correct answers. There may be more than one correct answer.

1 Tapirs are probably most similar to the
A cow.
B rhinoceros.
C elephant.

2 The tapir's existence is at risk due to the threat coming from
A hunters.
B tribes from other areas.
C other animals.

3 Luisa feels the greatest sense of pride from
A gaining support from the TCI.
B setting up her own business.
C communicating with older students.

4 Tapirs are celebrated by wildlife protection groups for their
A role in preserving the surrounding environment.
B similarity to particular animals on other continents.
C preference for existing in relative isolation.

8 Match the highlighted words in the article to the meanings.

1 a person or group of people with less power or money than the rest of society _____
2 a young person _____
3 someone or something that a lot of people are interested in _____
4 a socially valuable principle that is supported by some people _____
5 something that encourages a person to do something _____

Campaigning for a forgotten friend

Brazilian tapirs are the modern equivalents **(0)** _of_ a prehistoric species that initially lived in the northern hemisphere until moving south around 12,000 years ago. **(1)** _____ their distinctly strange appearance, there is something magical about these beasts, **(2)** _____ long noses are used to wrap around fruit, leaves and other food. Yet sadly, the tapir doesn't receive much in the way of admiration or appreciation. **(3)** _____ when compared to some of the more prestigious animals with **(4)** _____ the tapir shares a habitat – the jaguar and the caiman, for example – and this is a huge shame. And, while they are still classed **(5)** _____ vulnerable rather than endangered, there can be no doubt that the fall in **(6)** _____ numbers is greatly concerning. Young activist Luisa Guimarães has made it her mission to bring the message of tapir conservation and rescue to the wider world. After spending the last six years dedicating most of her free time, energy and passion **(7)** _____ her campaign, she has gained enormous credit from conservation organisations, winning prizes and awards **(8)** _____ the process. All this while still only 16.

At the start of year 6 in her school, she and her classmates were given a project to do on native Brazilian birds and beasts. Unsurprisingly, most people went for the well-known names: the anacondas, pumas, turtles and so on. Luisa, however, turned to a largely forgotten species: 'Most Brazilians have no concept of what a tapir is. Particularly in the cities, people have this mistaken idea that tapirs are some kind of inferior relative of the elephant or a weird-looking pig with a bendy nose.' To add to the confusion, anyone living close to tapirs in the Amazon rainforest or the Atlantic Forest is likely to call them *sachavacas*, which translates as 'bush cows'. The closest comparison you could make is with the rhino or the horse, 'so you could easily forgive the poor creatures for having an identity crisis,' she jokes. The main draw for her, in taking them on as the focus of her project, was that in Brazilian culture, tapirs are associated with a lack of intelligence. There, calling someone a 'tapir' is the equivalent to calling them an idiot.

Something about this situation spoke to her sense of injustice. She explains that, from a very young age, she had always been the type of person to favour and support the underdog, and this was no different. The more she investigated, the greater the knowledge she gained about how tapirs are being pushed further towards the endangered list. Habitat loss is, predictably, one of the biggest reasons for this development, as is the case for the majority of species across the globe whose existence is in question. Hunting has become a huge cause for concern. Luisa accepts that tapirs can provide a source of food for indigenous tribes. But it was finding out that tapir meat was increasingly being sold in commercial restaurants that gave her the incentive to start campaigning. 'Soon after completing my project, my family and I went to a new restaurant in the city and was horrified to see tapir on the menu,' she recalls. 'That night, I got straight on the internet and started looking into what I could do.'

She contacted wildlife organisations throughout Brazil to offer her help. Given her age – she was ten at this point – she was not immediately called in for an interview. However, the response was highly encouraging, particularly from a sympathetic contact at the Tapir Conservation Initiative (TCI). She praised Luisa for her desire to help the tapir's cause and suggested that the youngster aim to spread the word of what was happening and what could be done. Over the next three years, she made over 3,000 wallets, all of which she sold online, with all profits going to the TCI. It inspired her to keep pushing for change and, these days, she gives talks to hundreds of children at schools, scout groups and even universities. This has been her personal highlight – gaining the attention and respect of those whose place she aims to take in two years' time.

Due to living largely on their own, and with low rates of reproduction, tapirs are unavoidably susceptible to overhunting and habitat loss. They are enthusiastically referred to as the 'gardeners of the forest' by conservationists, as they play a vital role in the maintenance of healthy ecosystems. Tapirs becoming extinct in South America would be as devastating as losing the elephant in Africa or the kangaroo in Australia. There is a powerful argument that the success of campaigners like Luisa is equally as critical in today's world.

GRAMMAR
RELATIVE CLAUSES

1 Choose the correct options. In some sentences, both options are possible.

1 Hans Cosmas Ngoteya is a conservationist *whose / who* work I admire.

2 The teacher *to whom / whom* you would like to speak no longer works at this school.

3 My parents live in an eco-house, *whose / where* electricity is supplied entirely through renewable energy.

4 Anybody *who / which* gives their time to charity is a person to be admired.

5 The customer assistant *which / that* you need to speak to is not here at the moment.

6 Sugmundssen began to talk about his research trip to Antarctica, about *which / that* everyone was keen to hear.

7 My son, *who / that* teaches geography, has just been promoted to head of department.

8 In the rescue centre, there was clearly a mutual respect between the wildlife and the humans, *which / where* I found extremely interesting.

2 Complete the text by adding commas and the appropriate relative pronouns.

Environmental activism .... is growing in popularity throughout the world campaigns for the protection and repair of the Earth's natural environment. Campaigners .... are often in their teenage years regularly attend protests in the towns, cities and countries .... they live, drawing attention to the issues. That is not to say that they are people .... beliefs are limited to their home nation, and in fact they often travel the globe to visit countries overseas .... there are also considerable risks of damage and destruction. Today's environmentalists are determined only to stop .... governments and corporations agree to make drastic changes to the way they operate.

3 Correct the mistakes in the sentences or put a tick by any you think are correct.

1 Currently, there are over 120,000 species on the IUCN Red List, of that 32,000 are in danger of extinction.

2 Could you tell me about someone who efforts have made a difference to their local environment?

3 Young people today, about whom much has already been written, are the leaders of an environmental revolution.

4 Sales of commercial flights to space have angered climate activists, whom the inevitable pollution is unacceptable.

5 There has been a pause in the government's new Green Plan, to which the public were never consulted.

6 The community in where Helena Gualinga grew up has suffered greatly as a result of land exploitation.

4 Rewrite the sentences to make them more formal.

1 Endangered species, which there are a severely worrying number of, need our immediate help.
Endangered species, of which there are a severely worrying number, need our immediate help.

1 Climate change is a very real crisis which no one should be in any doubt about.

2 In my opinion, Greta Thunberg is someone we should all have huge respect for.

3 I've finished my volunteer application but I'm not sure who I should send it to.

4 Pietro's grandma, who he claims to get his determination from, was one of the first climate activists.

5 Isra Hirsi is a climate activist who it would be fascinating to spend an afternoon with.

5 Choose the correct options.

1 My biology teacher has always been someone *having / who has* a great belief in environmental causes.

2 How about we travel by train, *that / which* is less expensive and creates less pollution?

3 The desire to be famous is not a factor *which influence / which influences* young people to become climate activists.

4 All children *whom / who* are born at this time face an uncertain future.

5 People generally donate more money to causes they are interested *in / in it*.

6 For Greenpeace to achieve their goals, there are times *when / which* they have to work under huge pressure.

VOCABULARY
ADVERB–ADJECTIVE COLLOCATIONS

1 Complete the crossword with the adjectives that form correct collocations.

Across

3 virtually _____
5 rapidly _____
6 officially _____
8 randomly _____

Down

1 noticeably _____
2 naturally _____
4 universally _____
7 equally _____

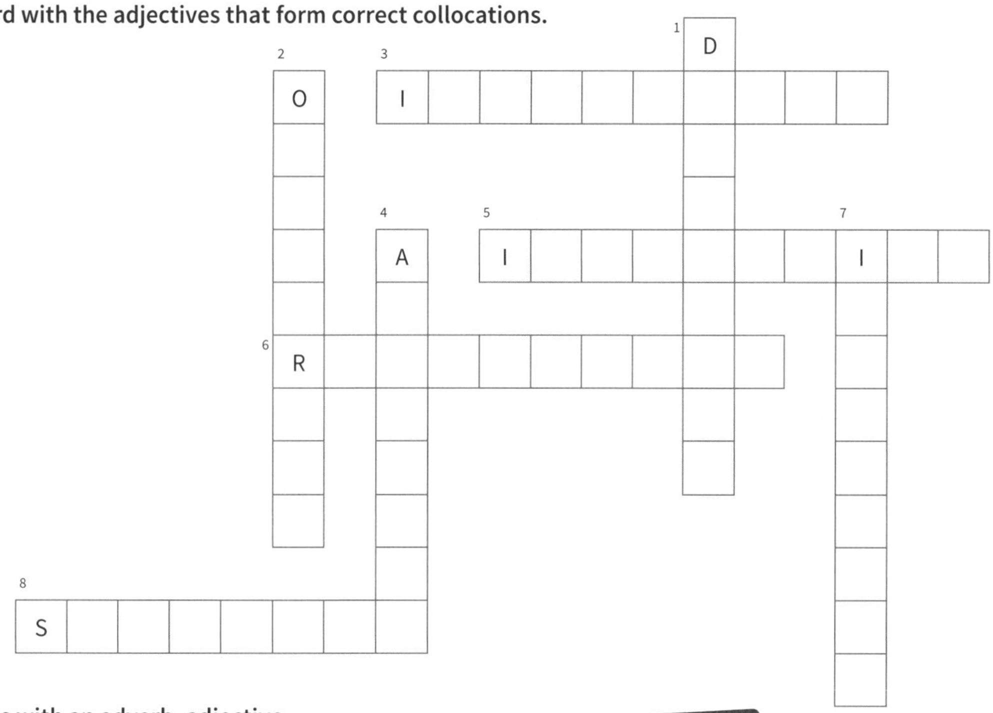

2 Complete the sentences with an adverb–adjective collocation from Exercise 1.

1 The African Grey, which is a parrot often kept as a pet, may soon be _____ by the WWF as *endangered*.
2 While habitat destruction has led to the disappearance of many different species, climate change has played an _____ role.
3 So many birds belong to the same species and yet are _____ from one another.
4 Photosynthesis is a well-known example of a _____ chemical reaction.
5 There are plans to test the latest treatment on 1,500 _____ people from an initial 5,000 volunteers.
6 It is _____ to reverse many of the effects of overfishing in our oceans and seas.
7 Scientists have announced emergency measures to combat the _____ destruction of the polar ice caps.
8 We need to agree on a _____ definition of the term *carbon footprint* before it can be effectively measured.

INTENSIFYING ADVERBS

3 Choose the correct options to complete the sentences.

1 Scientists have been _____ concerned for many years that we humans may not survive this century.
  A utterly   **B** deeply   **C** perfectly
2 Scientists were _____ disappointed that their panda breeding programme failed and no cubs were born.
  A bitterly   **B** fully   **C** dangerously
3 When I got to the site of the flood, the water level was _____ high, so I turned back.
  A highly   **B** utterly   **C** dangerously
4 Many marine animals are left _____ injured by the equipment used in the fishing industry.
  A bitterly   **B** fully   **C** seriously

4 Complete the sentences with the words in the box.

> aware   clear   cold   controversial   exhausted
> offended   underweight   unusual

1 You shouldn't make comments about other people's appearance as they could be deeply _____ by them.
2 I don't think that people are fully _____ of the dangers that climate change poses to humankind.
3 The link between climate change and rising sea levels is perfectly _____.
4 Every nation appears to be experiencing highly _____ weather this year.
5 Darwin's theory of evolution was highly _____ when it was first published.
6 After spending the past week volunteering at an animal sanctuary, I am utterly _____.
7 My uncle rescued and adopted a dangerously _____ dog he found abandoned near his home.
8 I enjoyed our day out hiking in the mountains. The only problem was that it got bitterly _____ in the evening.

1 Look at the photos. How do these actions affect the environment?

2 Look at some reasons (A–E) for taking action to help the environment. Listen to the first line of five monologues and try to match the reasons to the speaker.

A to experience a completely new situation
B to encourage further progress
C to compensate for a past action
D to improve a personal relationship
E to make a personal contribution

1 Speaker 1 …
2 Speaker 2 …
3 Speaker 3 …
4 Speaker 4 …
5 Speaker 5 …

3 Did you manage to match the options to the speakers? Why not?

4 Look at Task One in Exercise 6. Which of the options A–H do the sentences 1–5 suggest?

1 We didn't talk for days after, which really upset me. To make up with her…
2 I was suddenly furious they hadn't gone any further than that.
3 I couldn't go back and change what I'd done…
4 Who knows whether it'll make any difference in the long term, but I've got to try, haven't I?
5 I knew it would be something so unlike anything I'd ever done before – I just had to go…

5 Look at the options in Task Two. Option D is the correct answer for Speaker 1. Which of the three sentences (1–3) are you most likely to hear? Why?

1 I feel encouraged to make a more substantial contribution.
2 I was so impressed with their work that I'm now a volunteer on one of their patrol boats.
3 It's made me determined to play a more substantial part in protecting the environment.

6 Read the questions in Tasks One and Two. You will hear five short extracts in which people are talking about taking action to benefit the environment. For speakers 1–5, choose from the list (A–H). As you listen, you should complete both tasks.

TASK ONE

For questions 1–5, choose from the list (A–H) the reason each speaker gives for taking action.

A to experience a completely new situation
B to educate the local community
C to encourage further progress
D to compensate for previous activities
E to improve a personal relationship
F to become part of a global movement
G to learn from experienced campaigners
H to make a personal contribution

1 Speaker 1
2 Speaker 2
3 Speaker 3
4 Speaker 4
5 Speaker 5

TASK TWO

For questions 6–10. choose from the list (A–H) how each speaker feels after taking action.

A determined to adapt their future plans
B surprised to have reacted in a particular way
C frustrated by a lack of overall progress
D encouraged to make a more substantial contribution
E disappointed in the behaviour of neighbours
F unsure of the possible consequences
G convinced they can persuade others to make changes
H relieved to be free from expectation

6 Speaker 1
7 Speaker 2
8 Speaker 3
9 Speaker 4
10 Speaker 5

1 Which of the following options are correct?

The Cantabrian brown bear, as a species, will soon be *extinct / endangered / threatened / vulnerable* unless we take action.

2 Which of the following options are correct *now*? Why?

The Cantabrian brown bear, as a species, will soon be completely *extinct / endangered / threatened / vulnerable* unless we take action.

3 Read the article in Exercise 6 quickly. Then decide which of the following nouns are likely to be used in this context.

offenders   thieves   vandals   poachers

4 What meaning do the following words share?

A lowering   **B** declining   **C** dropping   **D** weakening

5 Which word from Exercise 4 forms a collocation with *population*?

6 Read the text and decide which answer (A, B, C or D) best fits each gap.

Rehabilitation of the Cantabrian brown bear

Not so long ago, the Cantabrian brown bear was close to being completely **(0)** *extinct* as a species, when as few as 60 remained in the wild. Not only had it become a victim of **(1)**_____ loss caused by deforestation, but it was also continually under threat from **(2)**_____ looking to sell their meat and fur, who carried out their criminal **(3)**_____ with very little intervention from the authorities. They were rarely even **(4)**_____ with a fine, not to mention sent to prison. It looked, to the casual observer, as if the only outcome the bears' **(5)**_____ population could hope for was to become exhibits in a museum.

In the 1990s, when the Cantabrian brown bear was on the **(6)**_____ of extinction, campaign groups began their attempts to re-establish its claim to survival. Today, these campaign groups **(7)**_____ the tourist market as a valuable source of income, encouraging bear-watching trips in the mountains of northern Spain. It is still officially **(8)**_____ as being in danger of extinction, but there is definitely hope for the future.

0 (A) extinct   **B** endangered   **C** threatened   **D** vulnerable
1 A home   **B** environment   **C** habitat   **D** surroundings
2 A offenders   **B** thieves   **C** poachers   **D** vandals
3 A tricks   **B** events   **C** movements   **D** activities
4 A provided   **B** sent   **C** issued   **D** given
5 A lowering   **B** declining   **C** dropping   **D** weakening
6 A margin   **B** boundary   **C** border   **D** verge
7 A direct   **B** target   **C** aim   **D** focus
8 A recognised   **B** recalled   **C** known   **D** remembered

7 Look at Exercise 9. Read the article quickly, covering the words in capitals on the right. Which of the missing words do you think you might already know?

8 Underline the correct options in the following sentence.

Half of all plant and animal species in the world's most *natural / naturally / nature* diverse areas are now considered at risk, with many now *dangerously / dangers / endangered* close to extinction.

9 For questions 0–8, read the text below. Use the word given in capitals at the end of some of the lines to form a word that fits in the gap in the same line.

Where do we go from here?

Half of all plant and animal species in the world's most **(0)**_____ diverse areas are now considered at risk, with many now **(1)**_____ close to extinction. Climate change has altered our world in so many ways, and it is impossible to turn back the clock on the damage that has been done. **(2)**_____, it is hard to imagine how we can stop it from developing even further, not when every day there is still such **(3)**_____ behaviour from individuals and governments alike. And certainly not while social media allows people to freely spread lies and **(4)**_____ about the long-term prognosis for the world. Many people deny that climate change even exists, while at the same time committing environmental **(5)**_____ on a vast scale.

NATURE

DANGER

WORRY

RESPONSIBLE

INFORM

VANDAL

Our world leaders often seem to be working in a completely **(6)**_____ way, blocking each other's plans for change and putting their own nation's needs first. We can only hope to **(7)**_____ the difficulties we face by agreeing on a plan and working **(8)**_____ together.

COOPERATE

COME

RESPECT

16 WHO DO YOU LOOK UP TO?

VOCABULARY AND READING
ROLE MODELS

1 Correct the mistakes in bold.

1 We may argue from time to time, but deep down, I've always **looked up at** my older brother.

2 Since seeing Arianna Grande in concert, I have **devoted myself for** becoming a professional singer.

3 I'm hoping my creative writing course will help me to **fill my ambition** of becoming the next George R.R. Martin.

4 When you don't follow popular thinking, you're always going to **push up against** challenges.

5 I joined the march because I wanted to help **raise awareness at** exploitation in the fashion industry.

6 My sister is the first person who inspired me to **campaign anti** animal testing.

7 To keep life interesting, I like to **throw myself towards** something new from time to time.

8 Having raised three children while also maintaining a successful career, my mum has always been a true **character model** to me.

9 I've always **thought widely of** my grandad, who has packed so much into his time and still lives such a full life.

10 I've been doing the same job for a few years now and it's time to **turn on a new challenge**.

2 Replace the phrases in italics with the corrected phrases from Exercise 1 with the same meaning.

1 Gene *gives all his time and effort to* helping people with no money or career prospects.

2 Most of my classmates *have a really favourable opinion of* our teachers, with one or two exceptions.

3 When he was at school, my grandfather *had to deal with* a number of teachers telling him that he wasn't clever enough to go to university.

4 There are a number of people in the public eye who children *respect, admire and want to emulate*.

5 When I decide to do something, I *do it actively and enthusiastically*.

6 I see it as my duty *to help people understand more about* poverty around the world.

7 Not everyone in the world can *do what they really want to do*, but there's no point in not trying.

8 My sister is the type of person who will always *push herself to do something difficult*, particularly if it involves physical activity.

9 Throughout her life, my mother has *tried to achieve success through planned activities to challenge* inequality in all areas of life.

10 You can't just decide to become a *person that others look up to and try to copy* – you get chosen to be one through your beliefs and actions.

3 Make notes to answer the following questions.

> celebrities   family members   friends
> politicians   sports stars

1 Do you have any role models from the categories of people above?

2 Which is the most popular category amongst you and your friends?

3 What makes these people good role models?

4 Read the four teenagers' reports on the opposite page quickly. Which categories of the people above does each writer refer to?

A _____   C _____
B _____   D _____

5 Read the reports again. For questions 1–10, choose from the teenagers (A–D). The teenagers may be chosen more than once.

Which person

1 disagrees strongly with a majority point of view?

2 suggests that not everyone is genuine in their choice of role model?

3 suggests a reason why focusing on appearances is pointless?

4 puts forward the idea that people's views can change as they get older?

5 questions an opinion about why role models are necessary?

6 believes that one particular outcome is the inevitable result of having a role model?

7 sets out a fundamental principle that a role model needs to follow?

8 defends their right to hold an unpopular opinion?

9 highlights the importance of identifying with the personal characteristics of a role model?

10 criticises certain people for encouraging confrontation?

Who do you **look up to?**

Four teenagers talk about who they admire and why.

A   Karen

There are a number of people who, perhaps because they want to come across as intelligent, supposedly look up to someone in politics. This would feel quite alien to me, as I feel that politicians, quite unpleasantly, often force people into a situation where they have to pick sides, and the last thing I want is to fall out with those around me. It's preferable for people to come together in their admiration for someone, rather than being divided. The movie or music industries are perfect for that. I admire the way that celebrities can inspire people even though they are just doing their job, and there are more than enough to keep everyone happy. Having said that, there have been many examples over the years of famous people behaving irresponsibly, and it's normal to question your connection to them when that happens. A couple of years ago, I'd have forgiven my heroes anything, but it's quite natural to mature in your outlook over time, and that's no bad thing.

B   David

There seems to be a dominant belief that all teenagers are obsessed with imitating their favourite celebrities, which I think is massively unfair. I'm not some mindless individual, tricked by social media into following and worshipping someone just because they're famous. I have – and I know that I'm not alone in this – a kind of 'mental check-list' that I refer to when evaluating whether or not I feel able to look up to someone. Like everyone in my family, I think highly of my grandfather, and not just because that's what you're meant to do, but because he's devoted to doing absolutely anything for anyone, even if he disagrees with them in some way. For me, accepting people for who they are is a non-negotiable starting point, so any role model of mine has to be entirely happy to show their compassionate side. I'm inspired by people who are good citizens or teachers, and by people who show total respect to others and to their choices in life.

C   Patricia

Obviously, famous people are often looked to for inspiration, but I could never call a celebrity a role model. They are primarily concerned with meticulously managing their image and spend so much energy constructing a picture of a perfect lifestyle. They do this despite the fact that perfection is such a subjective concept, so it's basically a waste of time. The fact is, so many people have completely unrealistic expectations about what and how much a role model can provide them with. For example, when someone with little or no money tries to imitate someone whose only defining quality seems to be their mind-boggling wealth. My grandmother once told me, 'live your life as your own role model', which I understood to mean that you should focus on living your best life – anyone that you look up to will ultimately be human, imperfect and bound to disappoint you. That's my interpretation, anyway. It might not be what people want to hear, but it's how I feel and I'm sticking to it.

D   Rodrigo

Many of my peers have a particular celebrity whose image and sense of style they imitate, believing that they somehow take on the qualities of that person just by owning the same clothes or shoes. That makes little sense to me. For example, if I wear an FC Barcelona shirt, it doesn't mean I suddenly acquire the talent or self-belief of an elite footballer. I truly believe that you have to see aspects of yourself reflected in a potential role model if you want to identify with them in a fundamental way; otherwise there would be nothing of substance to attach yourself to. I hope that some of my friends come around to that way of thinking at some point in their lives, and sooner rather than later. My mother jokes that without people to emulate, we'd only have ourselves to copy and it would be a disaster for society, so we need to find role models from somewhere, even if they are unsuitable for the job. That's fair enough to say in a light-hearted sense, but I hope she doesn't genuinely believe that. Role models are necessary, but I'd argue that they can't just be anyone.

---

6 Match the highlighted words in the article to the meanings.

1 not reasonable or understandable ....

2 respecting and admiring someone or something very much ....

3 strange and unfamiliar ....

4 in a way that shows great care and attention to detail ....

5 a person's way of understanding and thinking about something ....

1 **Choose the correct options.**

1 They walked together for three hours, *discussed / discussing* how their lives had changed since they'd last met.
2 Widely *admired / having admired* by fans, Pelé is one of the greatest football players in history.
3 *Waking up / Having woken up* at 4 am, it was no wonder he was feeling so tired.
4 There are a number of students in my college *expecting / after expecting* to do big things when they're older.
5 Yusuf has spent most of his life *dealing / dealt* with young people who have been touched by tragedy.
6 *Helping / Helped* throughout their careers by their family, the Williams sisters conquered the tennis world.
7 *Knowing / After knowing* that her parents were already in bed, she turned the front door key as quietly as she possibly could.
8 Ana is so confident that she'd go to any party without *worrying / worried* about not knowing anyone.

2 **Complete the sentences using the correct participle clause of the verbs below. Use the negative form where necessary.**

apply	be used to	~~expect~~
fail	hope	suffer	work

0 My grandfather stood with his mouth open, *not expecting / not having expected* the surprise birthday party that he had just walked into.
1 Hundreds of fans queued overnight at the movie premiere, _____ to see their heroes on the red carpet.
2 _____ from poverty as a child, she was determined to reach the very top of her profession.
3 My parents have spent their lives _____ to provide the best possible future for me and my sister.
4 _____ the way the movie industry works, he initially found it difficult to make progress, but is now greatly admired by everyone.
5 _____ to buy tickets to see the game live, we had to watch it on TV instead.
6 Peter Diamandis is an inspiring entrepreneur who has succeeded by _____ the same determination to every one of his projects.

3 **Correct the participle clauses in bold.**

1 **Had met never anyone famous before**, I was almost too nervous to speak. _____
2 When Marianna joined the Red Cross, her friends, **were always expecting her to do so**, felt a huge sense of pride. _____
3 **Rejecting by his parents**, the boy became determined to make his mark on the world alone. _____
4 The man Rico is speaking to is the one **teaches him** how to play the guitar. _____
5 After realising I had forgotten my homework, I turned around and ran back home, **felt annoyed with myself**. _____
6 **Stepped onto the stage to give his talk**, Jaime immediately wondered whether he had made the right decision. _____

4 **For questions 1–4, create single sentences by using the underlined verb to make participle clauses.**

0 Oprah Winfrey <u>was born</u> into poverty in rural Mississippi. She has never let her upbringing hold her back.
Born into poverty in rural Mississippi, Oprah Winfrey has never let her upbringing hold her back.
1 In her early career she <u>was based</u> in Baltimore. She hosted the chat show *People Are Talking*.
_____
2 *The Oprah Winfrey Show* was <u>launched</u> in 1986. It caused a sensation across the world.
_____
3 She ended her broadcasting contract in 2011. She <u>spent</u> more time on her philanthropic projects.
_____
4 She <u>has achieved</u> so much in her career. Despite this, she still works tirelessly on a number of projects.
_____

5 **Correct the mistakes in the sentences or put a tick by any you think are correct.**

1 Considering the list of candidates for the award, I have come to the decision that we should look elsewhere for the winner. _____
2 Comparing with most people her age, Billie Eilish has already enjoyed a remarkable career. _____
3 When I heard Malala Yousafzai talked about her experiences, it changed my outlook on life completely. _____
4 Having become an internationally recognised actor, Antonio Banderas is admired all over the world. _____
5 I would love the chance to meet Roger Federer, admiring him since I was a child. _____
6 After raised £20,000 to fund her invention, Alyssa Chavez was able to start producing the *Hot Seat*. _____

VOCABULARY
DEPENDENT PREPOSITIONS

1 Choose the correct options.

1 Being an elite athlete isn't compatible *for / to / with* having a social life; they've all made huge sacrifices in their personal lives.

2 Only recently has it become apparent *to / for / with* me just how important it is to set yourself goals in life.

3 I know I'm capable *of / in / to* becoming a professional actor, I just don't know whether I have the self-discipline.

4 Developing interpersonal skills is so important, especially since they are integral *in / to / with* most careers.

5 I have to admit, I was mistaken *in / with / of* thinking music college would be easy – it's really challenging me.

6 Cambridge is notable *to / for / in* its rowing facilities, but for most students, the early morning training sessions prove too difficult.

7 My father is my mentor, and I'll always be thankful *of / for / to* the opportunities he has given me in life.

8 I was utterly unaware *with / of / for* how long you have to work each day if you want to make it in the fashion industry.

2 Complete the sentences with the missing adjectives and prepositions from Exercise 1.

1 When I was ten, I was convinced I would be a movie star. Clearly, I was _____ thinking that this could ever happen.

2 Most people today seem to be _____ the ways in which online news can manipulate people into adopting a certain point of view.

3 Acknowledging your failures as well as your successes is _____ becoming the best person you can be.

4 My personal tutor is an amazing person. I couldn't be more _____ the support she has given me over the years.

5 The more I studied, the more I felt _____ getting good grades in my exams.

6 Mario's utterly irresponsible behaviour is in no way _____ the code of conduct we have at this football club.

7 From the moment she launched her YouTube channel, it was _____ everyone that she would make it to the very top.

8 Role models are often _____ donating lots of money to charity.

PHRASAL PREPOSITIONS

3 Create six phrasal prepositions using the words in the boxes.

| aside   contrary |
| in common   in the region |
| let   with regard |

| alone   from |
| of   to (x2) |
| with |

1 _____   4 _____
2 _____   5 _____
3 _____   6 _____

4 Complete the sentences with the phrasal prepositions from Exercise 4.

1 _____ banking and accountancy, there are a wide range of other careers available to maths graduates.

2 My brother has asked his teacher for advice _____ a career in education and what his next steps should be.

3 _____ my previous expectations, it was actually quite easy to find people in the music industry willing to offer their help.

4 I'd love to spend my weekends doing some volunteering work, but _____ most people my age, I am usually too busy with homework.

5 I'd love to be a professional footballer, but I couldn't cope with 10 minutes of intense physical activity, _____ 90!

6 In the media industry alone, there are _____ 500 different jobs you could go into.

5 For questions 1–8, read the text below and think of the word which best fits each gap. Use only one word in each gap.

How to motivate and inspire

A large percentage of people are mistaken
(0) *in* believing that no one could ever find them inspirational. They seem entirely unaware (1) _____ their potential to motivate others towards self-improvement. (2) _____ to this belief, however, the stories I have heard from so many 'ordinary' people seem to suggest we all are capable (3) _____ becoming a role model in some way. But how? First, being willing to show your true self to others is integral (4) _____ people looking up to you. No one likes a fake. Secondly, control your self-doubt. It isn't compatible (5) _____ what you're aiming to achieve. You don't have to be notable for a particular talent, (6) _____ alone have a name or face that thousands recognise. Just value yourself as you are. Finally, with (7) _____ to being a role model for everyone you meet – forget it. And don't worry about it. Even if only one person ends up thankful (8) _____ and inspired by the example you set them, you will have achieved something great.

6 Complete the sentences so that they are true for you.

1 Contrary to what some of my friends and family think, _____ .

2 In common with most people of my age, _____ .

3 Aside from _____ , the person I most admire is _____ .

4 I've always found it difficult to _____ , let alone _____ .

5 With regard to _____ , I most enjoy _____ .

6 In my life so far, there have been somewhere in the region of _____ that I _____ .

WRITING
A PROPOSAL

» SEE *PREPARE TO WRITE* BOX, STUDENT'S BOOK PAGE 123

1 Make notes for the questions below.

1 Do you recognise the person in the photo?

2 What do you think she does for a living?

3 In what ways could she be inspirational?

2 Read the task and make notes on who you would choose and why.

You read this announcement online.

A TV company, Flix TV, is planning to produce a series: *The World's Most Inspiring TV and Movie stars*. They would like viewers to send in proposals suggesting someone to feature in the series. Propose an actor, describe that person's contribution to their field and explain whether or not the person is a good role model for young people today.

Write your **proposal**. Write your answer in 220–260 words.

3 Read the proposal and compare it with your notes from Exercise 2.

The aim of this proposal is to provide a recommendation for an episode of Flix TV's new series on inspiring stars of the screen. There is a strong argument for the inclusion of Yalitza Aparicio, a Mexican actor who first became famous for her role in the critically acclaimed movie *Roma*.

Yalitza's career

When she won her breakthrough role as Cleo in *Roma*, she had never acted before. After being offered the part in her final audition, she informed the director that she had only just finished school and had been expecting to become a teacher. It is exactly this sense of modesty that has helped her gain a huge following worldwide. Not only was she just the fourth Latin American actress to be nominated for Best Actress in the Oscars, but she was also the first indigenous one. She has spoken extensively about how destructive stereotypes can be in preventing minority people from becoming successful. Featured as a cover star in a number of world-famous magazines, she has helped her community to become more visible. Indeed, she made it onto *Time* magazine's 2019 list of the 100 most influential people in the world.

Influence on young people

Young people today clearly understand the negative impact that stereotypes can have, both on individuals and on society as a whole. They can also easily look up to anyone who has managed to break down so many barriers. Yalitza has made history as an inspiring role model for so many, while at the same time keeping her feet firmly on the ground. In my view, there is no reason not to document Yalitza's rise to fame and ability to inspire others.

4 Look at these sentences from the proposal and underline the phrases that introduce a recommendation.

There is no reason not to document Yalitza's rise to fame and ability to inspire others.

There is a strong argument for the inclusion of Yalitza Aparicio …

5 Which of the following phrases are *not* suitable for introducing a recommendation in a proposal? Why?

1 If I were you, I'd …
2 It is highly recommended that …
3 I would strongly suggest …
4 You'd be crazy not to …
5 Without doubt, it would be a good idea to …
6 It's obvious that you need to look at …
7 It may be worth considering …
8 You totally, absolutely must …
9 There is certainly a case for …
10 There is no doubt that …
11 One possible solution might be …
12 Don't take this the wrong way, but …
13 It would be advisable to …
14 There's no point in doing anything unless …

6 Which four of the remaining sentences convey a stronger recommendation than the others?

7 Complete the sentences with the most suitable phrase for justifying a suggestion.

> As such   but it could also   in order to   not least
> so that   would ensure that

1 I would strongly suggest inviting local business leaders .... provide a solid networking opportunity for everyone.
2 Not only might this app encourage students to organise their homework more effectively, ... reduce the amount of paper used in college.
3 It would be advisable to keep an extra row of chairs at the back of the venue .... anyone arriving late does not cause unnecessary disruption.
4 A new community centre would serve a wide range of purposes, ... as a place for local elderly people to meet.
5 Uploading the course content onto a suitable platform .... all students can access the study material from home.
6 Rarely are goods paid for with cash these days. ...., I am in favour of moving to an entirely contactless payment system.

8 How do sentences 1–4 appear in the proposal in Exercise 4?

1 … said to the director, 'I've only just finished school and am expecting to become a teacher.'
2 She was the fourth Latin American actress to be nominated for Best Actress and the only indigenous one.
3 She has been featured as a cover star in a number of world-famous magazines. This has helped her community to become more visible.
4 After the director offered her the part in her final audition, …

1 ....
....

2 ....
....

3 ....
....

4 ....
....

9 Which grammatical structures are used in the answers in Exercise 8?

1 ....
2 ....
3 ....
4 ....

10 Read the question below and write your proposal.

You read this announcement on your school message board.

> The headteacher is inviting all students to propose someone that they admire at school to be given an award at the end-of-year assembly. You could propose a person such as a teacher, a peer or someone in a non-educational role in the school. Explain what the person does and why he or she is such a good role model for young people.

Write your **proposal**. Write your answer in 220–260 words.

Acknowledgements

The author would like to thank his wife, Alice, for her calm understanding and insightful support, and his two boys, Billy and Ronnie, for their less calm exuberance and unabashed enthusiasm for life, during one of the most demanding and unusual periods that will ever be thrown at us.

The authors and publishers acknowledge the following sources of copyright material and are grateful for the permissions granted. While every effort has been made, it has not always been possible to identify the sources of all the material used, or to trace all copyright holders. If any omissions are brought to our notice, we will be happy to include the appropriate acknowledgements on reprinting and in the next update to the digital edition, as applicable.

Key: U = Unit.

Photography
The following photographs have been sourced from Getty Images.

U1: wundervisuals/E+; Klaus Vedfelt/DigitalVision; Image Source; kali9/E+; Klaus Vedfelt/DigitalVision; **U2:** UlrikeStein/iStock/Getty Images Plus; FatCamera/E+; frantic00/iStock/Getty Images Plus; John M Lund Photography Inc/DigitalVision; Carlina Teteris/ Moment; **U3:** Tewan Yangmee/EyeEm; ER Productions Limited/ DigitalVision; andresr/E+; fizkes/iStock/Getty Images Plus; Pete Saloutos;

SolStock/E+; Andrew Brookes/Cultura; Charday Penn/E+; **U4:** Westend61; kupicoo/E+; electravk/Moment; ajr_images/ iStock/Getty Images Plus; Ridofranz/iStock/Getty Images Plus; Rawpixel/iStock/Getty Images Plus; **U5:** debela/DigitalVision Vectors; Monty Rakusen/Cultura; seraficus/E+; Giacomo Augugliaro/Moment; Andrew Bret Wallis/DigitalVision; Busakorn Pongparnit/Moment; izusek/E+; **U6:** Francois LOCHON/ Gamma-Rapho; Roos Koole/Moment; fotostorm/E+; Maskot; Donald Iain Smith; **U7:** BraunS/E+; Tim Clayton/Corbis Sport; Universal History Archive/Universal Images Group; Image Source/DigitalVision; martin-dm/E+; **U8:** Clarissa Leahy/ Cultura; Hill Street Studios/DigitalVision; Morsa Images/ DigitalVision; LaylaBird/E+; LordRunar/iStock/Getty Images Plus; BSIP/Universal Images Group; airdone/iStock/Getty Images Plus; Rawpixel/iStock/Getty Images Plus; guvendemir/ iStock/Getty Images Plus; SolStock/E+; **U9:** Yasser Chalid/ Moment; Tim Macpherson/Stone; PhotoAlto/Frederic Cirou/ PhotoAlto Agency RF Collections; monkeybusinessimages/ iStock/Getty Images Plus; Monty Rakusen/Cultura; **U10:** Peter Dazeley/The Image Bank; PeopleImages/E+; Hill Street Studios/ DigitalVision; Stockbyte; **U11:** Rubberball/Mike Kemp; ASIFE/ iStock/Getty Images Plus; BananaStock/Getty Images Plus; Ivan Pantic/E+; Shestock; Maskot; Johner Images; Fuse/ Corbis; dolgachov/iStock/Getty Images Plus; Pakin Songmor/ Moment; **U12:** PamelaJoeMcFarlane/E+; Dougal Waters/ DigitalVision; Ulrike Schmitt-Hartmann/DigitalVision; Marnie Griffiths/Moment; oleg66/E+; Westend61; **U13:** Klaus Vedfelt/ DigitalVision; ivosar/iStock/Getty Images Plus; Sarah Mason/ DigitalVision; Tim Robberts/DigitalVision; Portra/E+; Juanmonino/ iStock/Getty Images Plus; andresr/E+; Busà Photography/ Moment; Klaus Vedfelt/DigitalVision; SDI Productions/E+; Klaus Vedfelt/DigitalVision; SDI Productions/E+; **U14:** Peter Dazeley/ The Image Bank; John Lamb/Photodisc; grinvalds/iStock/ Getty Images Plus; Geber86/E+; OJO Images; Martin Diebel; kali9/E+; **U15:** johan10/iStock/Getty Images Plus; Images with heart and soul/Moment; Tier Und Naturfotografie J und C Sohns/ Photographer's Choice RF; Dgwildlife/iStock/Getty Images Plus; Wanida Prapan/Moment; sunlow/iStock/Getty Images Plus; Jose Antonio Espinosa/Moment; Carlos Davila/Photographer's Choice RF; JUSTIN TALLIS/AFP; shaunl/iStock/Getty Images Plus; Jorn/ The Image Bank; Grant Ordelheide/Aurora Photos; **U16:** Stuart C. Wilson/Stringer/Getty Images Entertainment; TPN/Contributor/ Getty Images Sport; Neustockimages/E+; Chip Somodevilla/Staff/ Getty Images News; FG Trade/E+; Tirachard/iStock/Getty Images Plus; Grosshans Grosshans/EyeEm; Bloom Productions/Stone;

Westend61; FangXiaNuo/E+; Lane Oatey/Blue Jean Images; Morgan Lieberman/Stringer/FilmMagic; Victor Chavez/Stringer/ Getty Images Entertainment; Hill Street Studios/DigitalVision.

The following photographs have been sourced from other libraries/sources.

U2: Photo 12/Alamy Stock Photo; Everett Collection, Inc./Alamy Stock Photo; Licensed By: Warner Bros. Entertainment Inc. All Rights Reserved. Reproduced with permission.

Front cover photography by oxygen/Moment/Getty Images.

Audio
Audio production by Leon Chambers at the SoundHouse Studios, London.

Typesetting
Typeset by emc design ltd.